25
32-34

51
61
67
74
95
100-101
104-105
120
122-123
125
128
141

# Reflections on the 1919 Black Sox:

## *Time To Take Another Look*

# Also by Gary Livacari

*Memorable World Series Moments* (2017)

*Paul Pryor: The Life and Times of a Twenty Year Major League Umpire* (editor, 2018)

# Reflections On The 1919 Black Sox:

## *Time To Take Another Look*

By

Gary L. Livacari

June, 2019

ISBN: 9781709112775

Printed in the United States of America

First paperback printing: October, 2019

# Dedication

This book is gratefully dedicated to my late friend, author Gene Carney, a great baseball researcher and the foremost authority on the Black Sox scandal. His book *Burying the Black Sox*, served as the impetus and inspiration for this project.

# Contents

# FOREWORD

by

Bill Gutman

There probably isn't a true baseball fan alive who hasn't heard of the infamous Black Sox Scandal of 1919. Many still consider it baseball's biggest black eye, a nefarious plot between gamblers and players to fix the World Series, a conspiracy that sullied the entire sport. The cast of characters features names like "Shoeless" Joe Jackson, Buck Weaver, Chick Gandil, Eddie Cicotte and Kid Gleason. When the highly-favored Chicago White Sox lost to the Cincinnati Reds in eight games, many an eye wondered if the great sport of baseball was indeed on the up and up.

It's no secret how it was resolved. Eight members of the Chicago White Sox were banned from baseball for life by the game's first commissioner, Kenesaw Mountain Landis. Thus the Black Sox were born and, some say, the game was saved. But was it really as simple as that? There's no doubt that gamblers were involved, no doubt that some money changed hands, and no doubt that the eight players banned from the game did meet with gamblers and each other to talk about "fixing" the Series. But did all that talk really translate to their play on the field? After all, no competitive athlete likes to lose.

With the 100th anniversary of this still memorable event upon us, baseball historian Gary Livacari has decided to take a look back, and he's done it in a most unusual way. Knowing that the scandal's centennial was approaching, the author decided to re-examine the Black Sox Scandal through a series of essays first published on his website: *Baseball History Comes Alive* (www.BaseballHistoryComesAlive.com). *Reflections on the 1919 Black Sox Scandal: Time to Take Another Look* is the result and will bring the reader back to 1919 to relive this World Series for the ages.

A century later, it's difficult to know exactly what happened, especially since no one really knew definitely back then. But there is enough evidence to raise some serious questions about what the players involved really did, how much money was dispensed and to whom, and whether the lords of the game manipulated both players and existing evidence in an effort to resolve the entire incident in their favor, and in the favor of baseball.

Mr. Livacari has researched the incident quite thoroughly—including its large cast of characters— and has organized the series of essays into a cohesive book. Reading it will not only allow the reader to know all the participants, but also draw conclusions about what actually happened and whether the resulting lifetime ban of the players by a commissioner given absolute and final power was fair and unbiased.

The author will not only introduce the reader to all eight White Sox players said to be involved, but to other players on that great White Sox team, including their manager, Kid Gleason. At the same time, he also takes a look at the opponents, the Cincinnati Reds, not exactly an inferior team in their own right, and their manager, Pat Moran. There are also essays detailing eyewitness accounts, the alleged eight suspicious plays that supposedly indicated a "fix," and what some of the players and writers who watched the Series unfold thought about the play on the field.

In addition, he will also focus on the games themselves, including star pitcher Eddie Cicotte's performance in Game One, when he was supposed to hit the first Reds' batter to let the gamblers know the fix was on. He did. And there's also a three essay arc on the most well-known player from that White Sox team, Shoeless Joe Jackson, who many feel should be in the Hall of Fame. Did Shoeless Joe really confess? Did his performance on the field indicate that he was giving it his all or letting up so his team wouldn't win? And what happened to the money Jackson was supposedly paid?

These are all intriguing questions that have never fully been answered. Based on the facts presented there's good reason to think that Jackson and co-conspirator Buck Weaver should be reinstated to the game, even now, long after their deaths. You'll learn the reasons, both pro and con, that have been debated for years. When you finish reading, as I did, you'll understand why this baseball moment, now 100 years old, continues to intrigue fans to this day.

I'm proud to have made a small contribution to the book, but in truth *Reflections On the 1919 Black Sox* is the brainchild and creation of Gary Livacari. He will bring you back to 1919 and give you a close-up look at what happened before, during, and after a World Series that will never be forgotten. And I guarantee he'll have you asking yourself a question that's never fully been answered, what really happened?

# Introduction

It always struck me as odd that there were conflicting views of what actually transpired between the white lines during the 1919 World Series. For instance, I always found it strange that the eye-witnesses, those who actually viewed the play in person, did not see any suspicious play. This included the umpires, the official scorer, the great majority of sportswriters, and the Reds players. In addition, there were thousands of fans in attendance over the eight-game Series and apparently they saw nothing unusual.

Christy Mathewson, on-hand in the press box looking for suspicious play, concluded it was impossible to "throw" a World Series. Reds' manager Pat Moran was quoted as saying, "If they threw some of the games they must be consummate actors, and their place is on the stage, for nothing gave us the impression they weren't doing their best."[1] Umpire Ernie Quigley noted that except for a couple spectacular plays, most notably one by the Reds' great centerfielder, Edd Roush, and another by Morrie Rath, the entire Series would have had a different outcome.[2]

Elliot Asinof's 1963 book, *Eight Men Out*, and the subsequent 1988 movie of the same name, written and directed by John Sayles, was the source of most of my initial information about the 1919 Black Sox scandal. I suspect this was the case for most baseball fans. The next step in my education came in 2006 when I read Gene Carney's book, *Burying the Black Sox*. I became friends with Mr. Carney and

[1] *New York Times*, October 1, 1920
[2] *The Sporting News*, October 7, 1920

corresponded with him numerous times about the scandal. We once went to a Cubs' game together at Wrigley Field when he was in town on a research project, and I took him to dinner, appropriately, at *Shoeless Joe's Sports Bar*.

As I read Gene Carney's book, I soon realized there was a lot more to the story than told in *EMO*. It also occurred to me that anyone relying solely on *EMO* for his or her information about the scandal would have only a superficial understanding of this sad chapter in baseball history.

Although an entertaining book, *EMO* lacked footnotes or any comprehensive sourcing. At one point Gene Carney interviewed Asinof and asked him if he regretted the lack of sourcing. He responded emphatically: "No! My sources were an amalgamation of hundreds of conversations, impossible to document."[3] Carney actually got him to admit that some of the stories in the book were fabrications. To be fair, Carney also noted that baseball books written before 1970 rarely had bibliographies, let alone footnotes. Which leads to the question, just how reliable is *EMO* as history?

Meanwhile, Gene Carney's book was heavily sourced and loaded with footnotes. In my opinion, it's the definitive book on the subject, even though it probably raised more questions than it answered. The point I took away from it was that there was much more to the story than the conventional wisdom had led us to believe. Most of the events of the scandal are shrouded in mystery and open to various interpretations. Many important aspects, like the 1924 Milwaukee trial, have been almost

---

[3] *Burying the Black Sox*, p. 24

completely overlooked.

Years went by, and then what really rekindled my interest was reading the 1956 *Sports Illustrated* interview of Chick Gandil by sportswriter Mel Durslag. In this fascinating interview, which is detailed in the first essay, Gandil made some startling admissions, including that he was a ringleader of the plot, and that the Black Sox got what they deserved. He never denied that the Black Sox conspired with gamblers to "fix" the 1919 World Series for a big payoff. All of his admissions of guilt gave his later claim that the fix was actually off by the time the Series started a ring of truth. In subsequent years, all of the banned players made similar statements. Yes, they conspired with gamblers and some took money. But no, they actually played the Series to win.

In the essay, I ask the question: "Is this the truth from a man near the end of his life trying to set the record straight? Or is he lying through his teeth one more time? If he was telling the truth—or anything close to it—then the 1919 World Series merits another look."

And that, in essence, is the theme of my book, *Reflections on the 1919 Black Sox.* What, exactly, does the contemporary, circumstantial evidence tell us? Is the conventional wisdom accurate, or is there more to the story than readers of *EMO* have been told? It's never been my intent to whitewash the involvement of the Black Sox, only to explore this sad chapter in baseball history in more detail. It's my conclusion that we don't know the complete story.

I've tried to uncover a bit more of the truth in this series of essays I've written over the past few years and have now compiled into a single volume. All the essays appeared on my Facebook page, *Old-Time Baseball Photos,* of which I am an administrator, contributor, and co-editor. They also appeared on my web page, *Baseball History Comes Alive* ([www.baseballhistorycomesalive.com](www.baseballhistorycomesalive.com)). Following this introduction and a detailed look at the Gandil interview, there are individual portraits of the eight Black Sox. These are followed by discussions of different aspects of the Series, including the accounts of the eye-witnesses; the seven suspicious plays recorded by sportswriter Hugh Fullerton; analysis of the play of Eddie Cicotte and Joe Jackson; the 1924 Milwaukee trial; and a look at the team that actually won the Series, the Cincinnati Reds. Many of the topics I chose to write about were mentioned in *Burying the Black Sox.*

I'm especially grateful to my friend, prolific author Bill Gutman for his support and encouragement. His contributions to this publication include the Foreword, plus essays on Commissioner Landis and star players Eddie Collins and Edd Roush. I'd also like to thank our resident baseball artist, Don Stokes, for allowing me to use his beautiful baseball colorizations.

My hope is that you'll find these essays interesting and of value to your understanding of the scandal that rocked the baseball world to its core in 1919. I also hope you'll agree with me that, after 100 years, it's time to take another look.

Gary Livacari

Park Ridge, Illinois

October, 2019

# One Hundred Years Later, Time to Revisit the Black Sox: The Gandil Interview

As the 100th anniversary of the 1919 Black Sox scandal approaches, maybe it's time to take another look. I recently reread the fascinating 1956 interview of Chick Gandil conducted by Mel Durslag for *Sports Illustrated*. Gandil was often cast as a ring leader of the plot to throw the 1919 World Series. Thirty-seven years later, at age 69, he granted the interview "against the better judgment of my wife," because, he said, there were things he wanted "on the record."[4]

Gandil seemed to be at peace with himself over his role in the scandal that had rocked baseball to its very foundation. This was baseball's darkest hour, and he had been at the center of the raging storm. Aside from embarrassment and personal qualms, he had never suffered any real hardship. Having worked for many years after his baseball career as a plumber, he noted that he and his wife "lived quietly

[4] *Quotes from Sports Illustrated*, September 17, 1956

away from the news." Apparently there were a still few details that he wanted to get off his chest.

What caught my attention in this interview was Gandil's repeated insistence that the 1919 Series was not thrown, and that all games were played "on the level," not exactly what the conventional narrative tells us. Gandil never tried to whitewash his involvement and made many striking admissions which had the effect of giving his claims a ring of truth. For instance, he confirmed that the Black Sox conspired with gamblers to "fix" the 1919 World Series; that he was a ring leader; and he conceded that he and his co-conspirators "got what they deserved." Regarding Judge Landis' famous decision, he termed it "unjust," but quickly added that he never resented it: *"Even though the Series wasn't thrown, we were guilty of a serious offense, and we knew it."* [Emphasis added][5]

Was Chick Gandil telling the truth? At this stage of his life, when setting the record straight seemed to be his objective, why would he continue to lie?

Has history given the Black Sox a "raw deal"? Certainly the eight conspirators—with varying degrees of guilt and involvement—initially made a devil's bargain with gamblers to throw the 1919 World Series. At least some of them accepted money. Gandil admitted this. But in the next breath, he emphatically denied the games were thrown, an entirely different matter. Here are his words:

"Our losing to Cincinnati was an upset all right, but no more than Cleveland's losing to the New York Giants by four straight in 1954. Mind you, I offer no

---

[5] Ibid

defenses for the thing we conspired to do. It was inexcusable. But I maintain that our actual losing of the Series was pure baseball fortune. I never did get any part of Rothstein's $10,000 and I don't know who did...*I give you my solemn word I don't know to this day what happened to the cash."* [Emphasis added][6]

These are strong words coming thirty-seven years after the fact. Either Gandil was "lying through his teeth," or history's version of the 1919 World Series needs to be reexamined.

According to Gandil, gambler Sport Sullivan approached him and Eddie Cicotte with the idea of throwing the World Series in return for a large payoff. When Gandil protested the feasibility of such a plan, Sullivan replied, "Don't be silly. It's been pulled before and it can be again."

They struck a deal which included "The Big Bankroll" Arnold Rothstein to throw the series for $100,000. The money was to be divided up among Gandil, Cicotte, and six other players of their choosing. They decided on Jackson, Weaver, Risberg, Felsch, McMullin, and Williams. They chose these teammates "to cut in on the gravy," not because they loved them, but "let's just say that we disliked them the least."[7] The eight players then greedily schemed to get even more money by making another deal with a completely different group of gamblers.

Now it got interesting. "The heat was on," said Gandil, as the Series drew near. Rumors of a fix were rampant. Some players received threatening phone calls and others started to panic. Sport Sullivan heard rumors that the deal was off and confronted

---

[6] *Quotes from Sports Illustrated,* September 17, 1956
[7] Ibid

Gandil, advising him, "I wouldn't call it the best policy to double-cross Rothstein." Gandil continued:

"I truthfully wanted to go to our manager Kid Gleason and tell him the whole story, but I knew it wouldn't be that simple. I realized that things were too involved by now to try to explain. I guess some of the others must have felt the same way, because the next morning I was called to a meeting of the eight players. Everyone was upset and there was a lot of disagreement. *But it was finally decided that there was too much suspicion now to throw the games without getting caught. We weighed the risk of public disgrace and going to jail against taking our chances with the gamblers by crossing them up and keeping the ten grand...Our only course was to try to win, and we were certain that we could.*" [Emphasis added][8]

Is this the truthful confession of a man approaching the twilight of his life, wanting to set the record straight? Is it the continuing distortions of a known liar and fixer, spinning yet another yarn? With a distance of ten decades, the issue can't be resolved with certainty.

The evidence supporting "crooked play" is threefold:

- The heavily-favored White Sox actually lost the series.
- The seven "suspicious plays" of Hugh Fullerton.
- The grand jury statements of Cicotte, Jackson, and Williams, characterized as "confessions."

The White Sox were heavily favored and losing certainly fanned the flames of suspicion. But the history of the World Series is replete with upsets:

---

[8] *Quotes from Sports Illustrated*, September 17, 1956

The weak White Sox of 1906 upset a great Cub team; the "Miracle Braves" of 1914 upset the mighty Philadelphia A's; the 1954 Giants upset the heavily-favored Indians. In more recent times, the Mets, the Marlins, and the Diamondbacks – teams barely out of their expansion years – advanced to the World Series and won. The White Sox' loss was not conclusive evidence of a thrown series.

And what about their opponents, the Reds? They were surely a strong team, led by Hall-of-Famer Edd Roush and star players Heine Groh and Jake Daubert. A later essay will discuss the Reds in detail. They had deeper starting pitching, as Sox ace Red Faber was out. In a nine game series, depth of pitching was key. And while they had deeper hitting, the White Sox were riddled with dissention and factions and entered the Series with heavy mental baggage.

The grand jury "confessions" of Cicotte, Jackson, and Williams were probably the most damaging to the Black Sox. Jackson's statement will be examined in detail in a later essay. But in the same statements, all three denied throwing any games, a fact rarely reported. Comiskey lawyer Alfred Austrian was reputed to have coached them, possibly fooling them into "confessing" under the false pretense of "getting the gamblers." In the 1921 trial, all three repudiated their grand jury statements.

Others have examined the statements and come to similar conclusions. Author James Kirby stated "they admitted agreeing to the fix with the gamblers and to accepting cash...but all three players also told the grand jury that they played the games to win."[9]

---

[9] *The Year They Fixed the World Series*, Feb. 1, 1988

Eliot Asinof had Austrian saying to Jackson, "To deny your involvement will prejudice the grand jury. Do you understand that?"[10] Gene Carney added "Jackson wanted to stay out of trouble so he testified. He said he let up some. And later, in the same statement, he said he played every game to win. In the newspapers the next day, no one reported the latter. Whatever Jackson said, it went down as a 'confession'."[11]

This interpretation of Jackson's statement focused the blame squarely on the players while shifting the spotlight away from Comiskey. But in the often-overlooked 1924 Milwaukee civil suit, Comiskey conceded that Jackson had played every game to win; and a jury voted 11-1 in Jackson's favor. The 1924 trial will also be explored in more detail in a subsequent essay.

Cicotte, like Gandil, admitted to guilt in the conspiracy—including taking money—but not to throwing the games. His remark "I did it for the wife and kiddies," is almost as famous as "Say it ain't so, Joe." Cicotte admitted intentionally hitting the first batter in the Opener, but then claimed he changed his mind, saying, "I pitched that best I knew after that. I lost because I was hit, not because I was throwing the game."[12]

Writer Victor Luhrs made the interesting point that Cicotte played the Series to win but, suffering pangs of conscience, was in "a bad mental shape as a result of his involvement with the gamblers. He was hardly fit to pitch the Opener."[13]

---

[10] *Burying the Black* Sox, p. 124
[11] Ibid
[12] *The Cleveland News*, September 29, 1920
[13] *The Great Baseball Mystery, by Victor Luhrs*, 1966

Isn't that exactly what Chick Gandil said in 1956? Luhrs also believed that Cicotte lied in his grand jury statement, and, as did Jackson and Williams, gave a version that was prepared for the eyes and ears of the gamblers.[14] Buck Weaver always maintained that he played his best and never took any money. He knew of the plot, but his only guilt was that he didn't squeal on any of the others. He had "guilty knowledge." Williams, Risberg, Felsch, and McMullin also made statements over the years indicating that they played the Series to win.

One hundred years later, is it still necessary for us to blindly accept the conventional wisdom without questioning it? Isn't the conventional wisdom in any field often proved to be wrong? Is it possible that the Black Sox—while certainly guilty of conspiring with gamblers and taking dirty money—could have played most, if not all, of the games "on the level"? Why would Chick Gandil be lying at this stage of his life? No one can say for sure, but my hunch is that the conventional wisdom does not tell us the complete story; and the idea that the White Sox played the Series to win remains a distinct possibility, worthy of further investigation.

This is not to exonerate the Black Sox by any means; but it's merely a suggestion that we need to assess the proper level of guilt. Conspiring with gamblers is less of an offense than actually throwing games. The prevailing version whitewashed the baseball establishment, which had turned a blind eye to the gambling scandal eating away at the game. Many of the Chicago and national sportswriters were Comiskey cronies—members of the famous Woodland Bards. They had a vested interest in

_____
[14] Ibid

minimizing the damage to his reputation and to the baseball establishment. We need to know the truth.

The Black Sox were an extraordinary mix of arrogance, stupidity, naivety, greed, and, yes, talent. Conspiring with gamblers to throw the World Series was a serious offense and they knew it. The acceptance of money irreversibly tarnished their reputations, and made their future protestations of innocence ring hollow. As with a tar baby, once they touched the gamblers, they could never break free.

I contend it's entirely plausible that, as the start of the Series approached, the thought of playing "crooked ball" was too much for them to mentally handle. Some cracked under the strain, as Gandil implied. The entire sordid episode was a blurred sequence of events where no one really knew what anyone else was doing. Conflicting stories were rampant. It's time to reexamine the events of the 1919 World Series with "pursuit of the truth" the only goal. Let the chips fall where it may.

# Spotlight on the "Eight Men Out": Ringleader Chick Gandil

With the 100th anniversary of the 1919 Black Sox scandal fast approaching, I thought it'd be a good idea to get a "head start" by featuring some of the most prominent players involved in baseball's darkest hour. I'll start, appropriately, by shining the spotlight on the supposed ringleader:

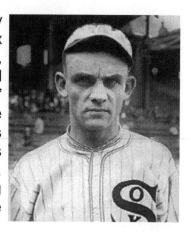

*"Are you crazy? We could never pull off fixing the World Series"* -Chick Gandil to gambler Sport Sullivan

*"Don't be silly, it's been pulled before and it can be again."* -Sport Sullivan to Chick Gandil[15]

While we often hear cries calling for the reinstatement of Shoeless Joe Jackson or Buck Weaver, there has never been any loved lost for Chick Gandil. No one ever thinks he got a "raw deal," only that he got what he deserved.

Described by his contemporaries as a "professional malcontent," the 6' 2", 195-pound Gandil had a

---

[15] All quotes in this essay from *Sports illustrated,* September 17, 1956

callous disposition to go with an intimidating mug. In his early years, he acquired his imposing physical strength working as a boilermaker in the copper mines, and later became a heavyweight boxer. Describing himself as a "rough, wild kid," he didn't hesitate to use his strength to get his way when necessary.

Gandil played 10 years in the major leagues with the White Sox (1910), Senators (1912-15), Indians (1916), and again with the White Sox (1917-19). Over his career, he hit .277, with 1176 hits, 556 RBIs, and 153 stolen bases. From 1912 to 1915, Gandil led the Senators in RBI three times. He was an excellent defensive first baseman, leading American League first basemen in fielding percentage four times and assists three times.

On February 25, 1917, he was reacquired by the White Sox. That season, the White Sox defeated the Giants in the World Series. In perhaps his first exposure to fixing games, Gandil and teammate Swede Risberg allegedly collected $45 from each member of the White Sox and paid off the Detroit Tigers in two crucial doubleheaders late in the season. The Tigers lost all four games, allowing the White Sox to win the American League pennant.

As the 1919 World Series rolled around, the gamblers, including Sport Sullivan, knew Chick Gandil would be safe to approach with the idea of a fix:

"I had only social contacts with gamblers until that September day in 1919 when Sullivan walked up to Eddie Cicotte and me as we left our hotel in Boston. I was kind of surprised when Sullivan suggested that we get a "syndicate" together of seven or eight players to throw the series to Cincinnati. The idea of a plot scared me, but he had a persuasive manner and backed it up with a lot of cash. He said he was willing to pay $10,000 each to all the players we brought in on the deal. Considering our skimpy salaries, $10,000 was quite a chunk, and he knew it."[16]

The fix was on, and it was eventually agreed that "The Big Bankroll," Arnold Rothstein would pay out $100,000 to the players. The money was to be divided up among Gandil, Cicotte, and six other players of their choosing. They decided on Jackson, Weaver, Risberg, Felsch, McMullin, and Williams. They chose the teammates "to cut in on the gravy" not because they loved them; but, according to Gandil, "let's just say we disliked them the least."[17]

In addition to serving as the contact for the gamblers, Gandil was responsible for delivering the cash. Although he later denied it, he allegedly received $35,000 for his role in the plot – nearly nine times his 1919 salary of $4,000.

The rest is familiar history. The heavily-favored White Sox lost the series and the eight conspirators were eventually indicted. In July, 1921 they stood trial for fixing the series. The jury found them not guilty, but their joy was short lived. Gandil and the others were permanently banned from organized baseball by new commissioner Kenesaw Mountain Landis.

In 1956, Gandil told his version of events to sportswriter Mel Durslag. Gandil admitted to leading the plot and expressed guilt and remorse over having done so. However, he claimed that after an

---

[16] Sports Illustrated, September 17, 1956
[17] Ibid

initial payment was made, the players panicked and ultimately tried their best to win. According to Gandil, they concluded they could never get away with it, and instead decided to betray the gamblers. Carrying all this mental baggage into the series, they couldn't play their best and eventually lost. It wasn't the first or last time a favored team lost a World Series.

Although he believed Landis' decision to ban them all was draconian, he felt they deserved what they got. Once word got out that they had conspired with gamblers and had actually accepted money, they were forever guilty in spite of what may have actually transpired on the field. From that point on, no one would ever believe their hollow protestations of innocence. Like a tar baby, once they touched the gamblers, they could never be totally freed.

Chick Gandil played semi-pro ball with other Black Sox teammates for a few years after the scandal. He eventually settled in the Napa region of Northern California and lived out the remainder of his life uneventfully working as a plumber. He passed away on December 13, 1970 aged 82, survived by Laura, his wife of 62 years.

# Spotlight On The "Eight Men Out": Buck Weaver

With the 100th anniversary of the 1919 Black Sox scandal fast approaching, I'll continue with a look at the "Eight Men Out," turning the spotlight today on George "Buck" Weaver.

*"Regardless of the verdict of juries, no player who throws a ballgame, no player that undertakes or promises to throw a ballgame, no player that sits in conference with a bunch of crooked players and gamblers where the ways and means of throwing a game are discussed and does not promptly tell his club about it, will ever play professional baseball."* -Judge Landis [18]

*"There are murderers who serve a sentence and then get out…Not me, I got life."* –Buck Weaver.[19]

Last January 18th was the 97th anniversary of a sad day in baseball history: On that day in 1922, Buck Weaver applied for reinstatement in professional baseball. Unfortunately, as we all know, his appeal was denied.

After "Shoeless Joe" Jackson, Buck Weaver, with his ever-present grin and his happy, optimistic

[18] Burying the Black Sox, p. 148
[19] Mike Downey, Chicago Tribune, article of October 20, 2005

disposition, is probably the most recognizable of the eight players banned for life following the 1919 Black Sox scandal. His suspension resulted from what was termed "guilty knowledge" rather than "crooked play." No one had ever suggested that Weaver gave less than 100% effort, batting .324, with 11 hits. He also played errorless ball, lending much credence to his lifelong claim that he had nothing to do with the fix.

Many baseball historians view Weaver's lifetime ban as a gross miscarriage of injustice. Yes, a case can be made that he deserved punishment for not squealing on his teammates as the World Series approached. He always claimed that this loyalty compelled him not to inform baseball authorities about what he had heard. But a lifetime ban for someone who gave his all and no one ever accused of "crooked play"? And was he the only one who had "guilty knowledge"?

Author Gene Carney, in his definitive book on the Black Sox scandal: *Burying the Black Sox*, repeatedly made the point that there were different levels of guilt in the plot. Instead, Judge Landis doled out a "one-size-fits-all" punishment. An appropriate punishment for Buck Weaver probably would have been suspension with eventual reinstatement. A life time ban from baseball now seems like a draconian sentence for his level of involvement.

Our contributor Kevin Trusty has rightly called Buck Weaver a sacrificial lamb. He shed some much-needed light on Buck's situation:

"Nobody *really* knew what was happening. Not then, and certainly not nearly a century later. It was for this uncertainty that players like Weaver kept their mouth shut during the Series. It was clear that there was some sort of problem on the field, but nobody was certain who was participating and who was playing honest. To make matters worse, virtually everyone within the White Sox organization had knowledge of it, but one man was crucified to take the fall..."[20]

Buck Weaver played eight years in the major leagues, all with the White Sox. Over his career, he hit .272, with 1308 hits, 421 RBIs, and 172 stolen bases. He started as a shortstop, but moved to third in 1917 when Swede Risberg joined the team. An excellent fielder, Weaver was known as the only third baseman in the league that Ty Cobb would not bunt against.

Weaver applied unsuccessfully six times for reinstatement before his death from a heart attack on January 31, 1956 at age 65. Later in life, Weaver contacted a New York City attorney who vowed to get him reinstated. Weaver sent his legal papers and correspondence to New York. They were never returned, and to this day, baseball historians have been unable to find Buck's legal files.

At the time of the 2005 World Series with the White Sox capturing their first championship since 1917, Chicago Tribune columnist Mike Downey implored Commissioner Bud Selig to rescind Weaver's ban. His column of October 20, 2005 cited Hall-of-Fame catcher Ray Schalk's condemnation of "the seven Sox" in on the fix, not eight.

Weaver's niece, Pat Anderson, told Downey: "I can't understand why someone would be so obtuse. Some of these commissioners, it's like they put a brown

---

[20] Post on *Baseball History Comes Alive*, August, 2018

paper bag over their heads."[21] Another niece, Marge Follett, came to the 2003 All-Star Game at U.S. Cellular to personally appeal to the commissioner for her uncle's reinstatement. So far, none of the appeals on Buck Weaver's behalf have been successful, and he remains "banned for life," even though he passed away 62 years ago.[22]

With this year being the `100th anniversary of the Black Sox scandal, let's hope the commissioner will take up the case of Buck Weaver and rightly rescind his unfair life-time ban.

---

[21] Mike Downey, *Chicago Tribune*, article of October 20, 2005
[22] Ibid.

# Spotlight on the "Eight Men Out": Eddie Cicotte

With the 100th anniversary of the Black Sox scandal fast approaching, I'm going to continue with my series on the "Eight Men Out." Today, we'll take a look at the career of pitcher Eddie Cicotte, with a beautiful featured photo of Eddie colorized by our resident baseball artist, Don Stokes.

*"I admit I did wrong, but I've paid for it the past 45 years."* -Eddie Cicotte, commenting in a 1965 interview on his role in the 1919 Black Sox scandal.[23] Eddie "Knuckles" Cicotte may be the most recognizable of the "Eight Men Out" after "Shoeless" Joe Jackson. His quote, "I did it for the wife and kiddies," is the second-most famous line associated with the scandal, right after, "Say it ain't so, Joe..."

Knuckleball specialist Eddie Cicotte pitched in the major leagues for 14 seasons. Over his career, he compiled a 208-149 record, with a 2.38 ERA, 249 complete games, and 35 shutouts, pitching for the

[23] SABR biography of Eddie Cicote by Jim Sandoval: https://sabr.org/bioproj/person/1f272b1a

Tigers, Red Sox, and White Sox. Sadly, had the scandal not terminated his career, Eddie may have made it to the Hall of Fame.

Eddie is also recognized as the first major leaguer to master the knuckleball. According to one description, "Eddie gripped the knuckler by holding the ball on the three fingers of a closed hand, with his thumb and forefinger to guide it, throwing it with an overhand motion, and sending it from his hand as one would snap a whip."[24]

Eddie made his big-league debut on September 3, 1905 with the Tigers. After a 3-year stint in the minors, he resurfaced with the Red Sox where he compiled a 41–48 record from 1908 to 1912. The Red Sox sold him to the White Sox on July 22, 1912.

He had a breakout year in 1913, going 18–12 with a 1.58 ERA. He topped these numbers with a great year in 1917 when he led the league in wins (28), ERA (1.53), and innings pitched (346). Eddie won Game One of the 1917 World Series, lost Game Three, and pitched six innings of relief in Game Five. Injuries reduced him to a 12–19 record in 1918; but in 1919 he rebounded to an outstanding 29-7 record (.800) and again led the league in wins, winning percentage (.806), innings pitched (306), and complete games (30).

Eddie reportedly resisted repeated attempts by Chick Gandil to join in the plot to throw the 1919 World Series until just days before the Series opened. He pitched in three games, winning one, but pitched ineffectively and lost the other two. Probably the most famous pitch he ever threw was the one that nailed

---

[24] Ibid.

Cincinnati Reds leadoff man Morrie Rath squarely in the back to lead off the 1919 World Series—a pitch that signaled to the gamblers that the fix was on.

Eddie Cicotte was the first of the eight players to come forward admitting guilt, signing a confession and a waiver of immunity. He later recanted this confession and was acquitted of all charges at the jury trial. But the joy was short lived, as Judge Landis permanently banned Eddie and the seven other Black Sox for life.

After the scandal, Eddie returned to Livonia, Michigan, where he managed a service station and later became a game warden. He also worked for the Ford Motor Company, retiring in 1944. At the time of his death on May 5, 1969 at age 84, he was a strawberry farmer in Farmington, Michigan. In an interview in 1965, he said he lived his post-baseball life quietly. He agreed that he had made mistakes, but insisted that he had tried to make up for it by being a good husband and father, and living as clean a life as he could after baseball.

We're all responsible for the decisions we make in life—some of them with better results than others. Unfortunately, Eddie Cicotte made a bad one back in 1919; and he had to live with the consequences for the rest of his life.

# Spotlight on the "Eight Men Out": Oscar "Happy" Felsch

*"Well, the beans are spilled and I think I'm through with baseball. I got $5,000. I could have got just about that much by being on the level if the Sox had won the Series. And now I'm out of baseball — the only profession I know anything about, and a lot of gamblers have gotten rich. The joke seems to*  *be on us."* –Oscar "Happy" Felsch[25]

I'm continuing my series on the eight ball players banned for life from baseball by Commissioner Landis in the wake of the 1919 Black Sox scandal. Today we turn our attention to the White Sox' star center fielder, Oscar "Happy" Felsch

Hap Felsch, who picked up his nickname early in life from his smiling, easy-going demeanor, played center fielder for the White Sox from 1915 to 1920. He was born in Milwaukee, Wisconsin, to German immigrant parents and began his professional baseball career in the Wisconsin-Illinois League in 1913. The next season, he batted .304 for the American Association Milwaukee Brewers, and was

[25] SABR biography of Oscar Happy Felsch, by Jim Nitz: https://sabr.org/bioproj/person/cd61b579

purchased by the White Sox.

Over his career, Felsch hit .293 with 38 home runs, and 448 RBI. His last season in the majors, 1920, was his best. He hit .338 with 14 home runs and 115 RBI. It's likely he would have put up more big numbers in the live-ball era had he not received a lifetime ban.

From 1916 to 1920, Felsch was one of the best hitters in the American League, batting over .300 three times, and finishing in the top-10 in numerous offensive categories. His 102 RBI in 1917 was good for second place, as the White Sox won the American League pennant and World Series. He missed most of the 1918 season due to military service.

Felsch continued his good hitting and fielding in 1919. He had a strong throwing arm and was regarded as an outstanding center fielder. He led the American League in outfield putouts and assists in 1919, as a strong White Sox team won another pennant.

That fall, Felsch joined a group of eight White Sox players that allegedly plotted to intentionally throw the 1919 World Series. He was reluctant to go along at first, but then eventually did because of the promised payoff. For his part in the fix, Felsch admitted receiving $5,000, which was more than his entire regular season salary of $2,750. After the scandal broke in late 1920, Felsch, along with seven other players, was banned from baseball by Commissioner Landis. Later, he admitted his knowledge of the plot and admitted taking money; but, similar to statements made by other implicated players, he denied he was involved in throwing any games.

Was he lying? Was he really not involved in "crooked

play" as he and the other accused players claimed? We'll never know for sure. But, in a point I've made many times, once it became known that the players had conspired with gamblers to throw the Series and money was actually given and accepted, their protestations of innocence forever rang hollow. Once they consorted with gamblers to this degree, and money was accepted, then, like a tar-baby, they could never break free. All of them, with the possible exception of Buck Weaver, who took no money and gave one hundred percent on the field, seemed to realize this. Most stated at one time or another that they got what they deserved, regardless of what actually happened on the field.

Felsch told the story of his part in the scandal on September 29, 1920. He largely substantiated the confessions made by Cicotte and Jackson; and in expressing regret for his action, said he saw nothing left in life for him. In 1925, Felsch, Risberg, and Jackson sued the White Sox for back pay. On February 9, 1925, he was awarded $1,166 in salary plus interest in a suit alleging breach of contract.

Felsch spent the next 15 years touring the country with various amateur and semi-pro teams, including the Scobey, Montana Outlaws in 1925 and 1926; Regina Balmorals of the Southern Saskatchewan Baseball League in 1927; and in Plentywood, Montana in 1928. After his playing days ended, he opened up a grocery store as well as a number of drinking establishments. He was also a crane operator.

Oscar "Happy" Felsch died of a liver ailment in Milwaukee in 1964, just five days before his 73rd birthday

# Spotlight on the "Eight Men Out": Swede Risberg

*"The Swede is a hard guy."* –Shoeless Joe Jackson[26]

Swede Risberg was a 25-year-old rising young star in the American League when he was banned for life following his participation in the

Black Sox scandal. He was the youngest of the eight White Sox players banned by Judge Landis.

Swede made his major league debut with the Sox on April 11, 1917. A converted pitcher, he was a below-average hitter, but he won the starting shortstop job due to his outstanding defensive skills and his cannon of an arm. Over his career (1917-'20) all with the White Sox, he hit .243 with 175 RBI.

Risberg missed a good chunk of the 1918 season, as did many players, working in a shipyard as part of the war effort. The job was considered essential, and served a useful purpose: Even though it consisted largely of playing baseball, it kept him out of the draft. He was back with the Sox for the pennant-winning 1919 season. He hit .256 and drew raves for his strong arm and stellar defense as the Sox cruised to their second pennant in three years.

---

[26] SABR biography of Swede Risberg by Kelly Boyer Sagert and Rod Nelson: https://sabr.org/bioproj/person/fde3d63f

The Sox were a divided team with two distinct cliques: the first consisted of the educated players, centering around Columbia grad Eddie Collins. The other might be called, for lack of a better term, "the rowdies," with Chick Gandil calling the shots. Unfortunately, Risberg ran with the latter group. They thought they were underpaid by cheapskate owner Charles Comiskey; and so, the story goes, they devised a plan to throw the 1919 World Series. The payoff? An enticing ten grand each.

The Swede was not a nice guy; and, like Gandil, definitely not someone you wanted to mess with. Also like Gandil, there has never been a movement to have Swede Risberg reinstated. The sentiment has always been that he got what he deserved.

He was reportedly one of the ringleaders of the nefarious plot and also filled the role of enforcer, helping to "convince" some of the others to go along with the scheme. Once in, it fell to him to keep the others in line. In a court deposition, Joe Jackson said that when he didn't receive his promised money and threatened to expose the plot, Risberg, mincing no words, actually threatened to kill him if he blabbed. Apparently, Jackson didn't think Swede was kidding and got the message.

Here's sportswriter Hugh Fullerton's assessment of the Swede:

"He is liable to be a sensation one minute and a crape-hanger the next, for he can throw them away as far and as hard as anyone. The boy is high strung, nervous, and inclined to panic. ... His fault is that he seems striving constantly to conceal his nervousness under a veneer of pretended toughness."[27]

Risberg's play during the Series against the Reds tended to severely undermine his later protestations of innocence, as he hit an anemic .080 and committed four errors. He later claimed that he was bothered by a bad cold. Risberg was acquitted in the ensuing trial, but then was banned for life by Commissioner Kenesaw Mountain Landis along with his seven implicated teammates. Risberg continued to play semi-pro baseball for a decade after his banishment.

In 1926, Risberg was called to testify about a 1917 gambling scandal involving Ty Cobb and Tris Speaker. Although he presented no evidence regarding this scandal, he claimed that in 1917 he had collected money from other White Sox players to pay off the Tigers to intentionally lose games. However, his story was contradicted by many others and was disregarded.

After his outlaw baseball career ended, Swede eventually ran a tavern and lumber business in the northwest United States. During his playing days, he had once been badly spiked by an opposing player. The injury never properly healed and the leg was eventually amputated.

At the end of his life, he lived with his son and remained an avid baseball fan. He was the last surviving Black Sox player. Risberg always refused to discuss his role in the Black Sox scandal. He died in a convalescent home in Red Bluff, California in 1975 on his 81st birthday.

---

[27] SABR biography of Swede Risberg by Kelly Boyer Sagert and Rod Nelson: https://sabr.org/bioproj/person/fde3d63f

# Spotlight on the "Eight Men out": Shoeless Joe Jackson

*"Say it ain't so, Joe"–* Famous quote, probably apocryphal, from *Eight Men Out*

There's probably no topic that's more emotionally charged when discussing the Black Sox scandal than Joe Jackson's guilt or innocence. It's still hotly debated almost 100 years later. The best analysis of his role in the sordid affair can be found in Gene Carney's highly acclaimed book, *Burying the Black Sox,* which I highly recommend.

It's true that Jackson made an original incriminating grand jury statement. This statement has probably done the most lasting damaging to his reputation; but as Mr. Carney states, this statement should be characterized as a "contradictory account of a confused witness." Often overlooked is that he repeatedly added in the same statement that he played all games to win.

In the 1924 civil trial brought by Jackson against Charles Comiskey for breach of contract and back pay, eleven of twelve jurors believed Jackson had played every game to win, and that he had not been in on the conspiracy. Unfortunately for Jackson, the jury verdict was overturned by the judge who could not overlook the contradictions with his 1920 grand jury statement.

We won't settle his guilt or innocence here, so let's take a look at the career of this great hitter, especially his three-year span from 1911-1913.

Joe Jackson is usually remembered for his great years with the White Sox from 1915 to 1920 and for his remarkable .356 career batting average, which is still the third-highest all-time. It's well known that Babe Ruth modeled his hitting technique after Jackson's.

But few realize that Shoeless Joe had some truly remarkable years earlier in his career with the Cleveland Naps. His rookie year of 1911 is "off the charts" for a rookie; and his three-season totals from 1911-1913 is arguably one of the best three-year spans in baseball history.

Joe's stats from 1911 would be amazing even if he wasn't a rookie. He compiled 233 hits, with 126 runs, 45 doubles, 19 triples, 83 RBIs, and 41 stolen bases. His phenomenal .408 batting average set a record for rookies that still stands and we can safely say will never be broken. Incredibly, it was only good enough for second in the league behind Ty Cobb's .420. It's still the sixth-highest single-season total since 1901. His .468 on-base percentage led the league, and he posted a .590 slugging average. Truly a remarkable season.

It's hard to imagine how one could improve on a season like that, but he came close in 1912. That year Jackson's batting average "slumped" to .395, but he led the American League in hits (226), triples (26), and total bases (331). He also collected 44 doubles, 90 RBIs, 35 stolen bases, a .458 on-base percentage, and a .579 slugging average.

Jackson's phenomenal run wasn't finished. The next year, 1913, may have been the best of the three. His 197 hits, 39 doubles, and .551 slugging percentage all led the American League. He hit .373 for the year, with 71 RBI, 17 triples, 26 stolen bases, 291 total bases, and a .460 on-base percentage. Jackson struck out only 26 times in 623 at-bats.

Over this three-year span, from 1911 to 1913, Joe Jackson's batting average was .392, with an average per year of 218 hits, 118 runs scored, 42 doubles, 21 triples, 81 RBI, and 34 stolen bases. In 1999, he ranked number 35 on The Sporting News list of the 100 Greatest Baseball Players and was a finalist for the Major League Baseball All-Century team. Fans voted him as the 12th-best outfielder of all-time. He also currently ranks 33rd on the all-time list for non-pitchers according to the win shares formula developed by Bill James.

Shoeless Joe's involvement in the scandal will be examined in more detail in subsequent essays.

# Spotlight on the "Eight Men Out": Claude "Lefty" Williams

"Anything they did would be agreeable to me if it was going to happen anyway…I had no money and I might as well get what I could." –Lefty Williams[28]

The Black Sox scandal rocked the baseball world to its core in 1919. There were many personal tragedies associated with this, the most sordid chapter in baseball history; but none more so than the story of Claude "Lefty" Williams.[29]

By 1919, the 26-year-old pitcher was a budding star whose best years seemed to lie just ahead. But, as is well known, he made one very bad decision which effectively brought an end to a promising career. Like others involved in the fix, Lefty lived the rest

[28] Boston Globe, September 29, 1920, 16.
[29] Information on Lefty Williams and quotes from SABR biography written by Jacob Pomrenke: https://sabr.org/bioproj/person/0998b35f

of his life tormented by the eternally unanswerable question: "What might have been?"

By the time of his banishment, he was just entering his prime. After seven seasons in the Big Show, Lefty had compiled a remarkable 82-48 record with a 2.31 ERA. His .631 winning percentage still ranks in the top-25 all-time among American League pitchers. Nearly a century later, no other American League pitcher had recorded more wins in his final active season than Lefty's 22 in 1920.

Lefty began his major league career in 1913 with the Tigers. After a couple stellar minor league seasons, he caught the attention of the White Sox. They picked him up in 1915, and by 1916 he had settled into their starting rotation. Possessing outstanding control, a mid-nineties fastball, and a swooping curve, he helped the White Sox win the pennant in 1917 with an excellent 17–8 record (.680).

Like many ballplayers during World War I, Lefty missed most of the 1918 season, appearing in only 15 games. He spent most of the year working in Navy shipyards in support of the war effort. He came back strong in 1919 with his best season, 23–11 (.676) with a 2.64 ERA, as the White Sox again won the American League pennant. He led the American League that season with 40 starts and was second with 27 complete games.

His baseball fate became forever sealed shortly before the start of the 1919 World Series when teammate Chick Gandil approached him outside the Ansonia Hotel in New York. Gandil offered the underpaid Lefty a cool ten grand to participate in the World Series "fix." With a salary of only $2,600, it apparently was an offer he couldn't refuse.

His piece of the action never fully materialized, however, as he only saw five grand—just half of his promised cut of the dough. Ironically, the five-grand payoff was about the same he would have received had the Sox had won the World Series.

With rumors of a fix already in the air, Lefty immediately raised suspicions in Game Two with an uncharacteristically wild performance. He starting the game by facing the minimum nine batters through the first three innings, but then unexplainably slipped into wildness in the fourth. He surrendered only four hits but walked six (tying a career high), as the Sox fell 4-2 and went down 0-2 in games.

Another disastrous inning proved to be his downfall in Game Five, resulting in a 5-0 loss. After allowing just one hit through five innings, Lefty gave up four runs in the sixth. His poor performance in Game Eight, the final game of the series, where he lasted less than an inning pitching to all of five batters, is well known.

For the series, Lefty went 0–3, with a 6.63 ERA. His three losses set a World Series record for futility that stood until 1981. Lefty later claimed he was unable to fully concentrate with the fix playing prominently on his psyche: "I was sorry. I wanted to be out of it and not mixed up in it at all."[30]

There were conflicting views of Lefty's poor performance in Game Two. Catcher Ray_Schalk suspected something wasn't right with Williams who

[30] Information on Lefty Williams and quotes from SABR biography written by Jacob Pomrenke: https://sabr.org/bioproj/person/0998b35f

lacked his normally sharp control. Schalk had words with Lefty after the game which some say evolved into fisticuffs. *Chicago Tribune* sportswriter Irving Sanborn saw it the same way, writing that Lefty was almost criminally wild.

But home plate umpire Billy Evans had a different take: "I regarded the loss of that game at the time as one of the hardest bits of luck I ever saw. All of the fourth-inning walks were on full counts and not one of them was over six inches inside or outside."[31]

After Game Four, Gandil gave Lefty $10,000, half of which was to go to Joe Jackson. Lefty famously delivered "the goods" to Jackson under his pillow in a dirty envelope. The players were now deeply bound to the gamblers; and like a tar baby, could never break free.

In 1920, Williams went 22–14, but was named in the indictments handed down by the Cook County Grand Jury. Though acquitted in the subsequent trial, Williams and the seven other Black Sox were banned for life by Judge Landis.

With baseball being the only life he really knew, Williams barnstormed and played in outlaw leagues for a few years. In 1922, he joined up with Swede Risberg, Buck Weaver, and Happy Felsch on a short-lived team promoted as the "Ex-Major League Stars," which toured the Midwest playing town teams in Illinois, Wisconsin, and Minnesota.

Here's some interesting information about Lefty Williams from his SABR biography:

"More than any other player involved in the 1919

---

[31] Ibid.

World Series fix, Williams struggled to make peace with his fateful decision to accept the bribe. Like many players of his era, he had few other marketable skills outside of his ability to play baseball. After struggling to run a pool hall on Chicago's South Side…Williams took odd jobs as a painter, a department store floor man, and a tile-fitter...He began drinking more and his marriage suffered...In 1923, with Lefty still drinking heavily, his wife Lyria kicked him out of the house and the couple separated." [Ed. note: They later reconciled and Lyria played a major role in straightening out his life].[32]

Lefty Williams spent his later years in Laguna Beach, California, operating a garden nursery business. He passed away on November 4, 1959, ironically just weeks after the White Sox—with their first pennant since the Black Sox scandal of 1919—lost the World Series to the Dodgers.

---

[32] Information on Lefty Williams and quotes from SABR biography written by Jacob Pomrenke: https://sabr.org/bioproj/person/0998b35f

# Spotlight on the "Eight Men Out": Fred McMullin

Today we turn our attention to the eighth and perhaps the most obscure of the "Eight Men Out," Fred McMullin. He's not better known because he was a utility player in 1919 with only two at-bats in the infamous World Series, going 1-2 with a single.

Fred McMullin was born on October 13, 1891 in Scammon, Kansas. He played six seasons in the major leagues for the Tigers (1914) and White Sox (1916-1920). Over his career he hit .256 with one home run and 72 RBI. He had remarkable success as a base stealer, swiping 31 bags in 32 attempts. His best season was the fateful year of 1919 when he hit .297 in 60 at-bats with a .355 on-base percentage.

The light-hitting McMullin had played a key role in the 1917 World Series victory. A pivotal player in the White Sox' stretch run to clinch the pennant, he drove in the first run of the World Series; and while he went only 3-24 at the plate, he played flawless defensive which included at least two spectacular plays.

McMullin was "tight" with conspirators Swede Risberg and Chick Gandil and was said to have eavesdropped his way into the plot to "fix" the 1919 World Series. He overheard conversations about it in the White Sox locker room and insisted on a "piece of the action." Apparently, he even threatened to "blow the whistle" unless he was included. It's also possible he heard about the plot from his drinking buddy, the shady gambler, Billy Maharg. Other reports have him as one of the instigators of the plot. Eddie Cicotte testified that the idea of the fix had originated in a conversation with Gandil and McMullin.

Fred McMullin served as Chicago's advance scout for the 1919 World Series, which may explain how and why he earned an equal share in the payout ($5,000) from the fix. Some historians have suggested that, as a means to cover himself and his co-conspirators, McMullin delivered a flawed scouting report to all the "clean" Sox about what to expect from Cincinnati's pitchers. That notion has never been verified.

With only two at-bats in the series, he had little chance to do any "fixing." He was not included in any of the "Seven Suspicious Plays" of sportswriter, Hugh Fullerton. Nevertheless, for his role in the conspiracy, McMullin was banned for life, along with seven of his teammates, by Commissioner Kenesaw Mountain Landis.

According to his SABR biography, Fred McMullin's story is a series of contrasts:

"A man once commended for chasing gamblers off a field in Boston, he was suspended permanently because he accepted a $5,000 bribe to help his team lose. He was indicted by a Chicago grand jury in a story that made headlines across the nation, yet he spent the final decade of his life as a respected lawman in California."[33]

McMullin never spoke publicly about the Black Sox scandal. After baseball, he held numerous jobs throughout his life such as a carpenter, office jobs, traffic manager and Los Angeles County deputy marshal. McMullin's final years were plagued by ill health caused by arteriosclerosis. On November 19, 1952, just over a month after his 61st birthday, he had a fatal stroke. McMullin was buried at Inglewood Park Cemetery.

[33] SABR biography of Fred McMullen by Jacob Pomrenke: https://sabr.org/bioproj/person/7d8be958

# 1919 Cincinnati Reds: Talk About Being Overshadowed!

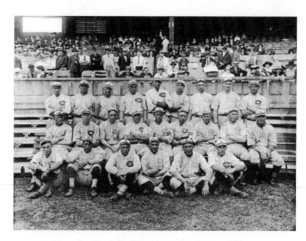

"If they threw some of the games they must be consummate actors, and their place is on the stage, for nothing gave us the impression they weren't doing their best." -Reds' manager Pat Moran [34]

Those of you following along with my posts about the 1919 World Series, know where I stand. As I've said many times, I don't know what really happened, but my hunch is that the conventional wisdom doesn't tell the whole story.

Were the Black Sox guilty of cavorting with gamblers, agreeing to a "fix," and accepting money? Yes, for sure. Did they get what they deserved? Most definitely. Did they actually throw World Series games? Well, of that I'm still not so sure.

I've recently been thinking about the team that actually won the Series: the Cincinnati Reds. "Upon

---

[34] *The New York Times*, October 1, 1920

further review," I've come to the conclusion that the Reds were a pretty darn good team. Read on and see if you agree with me...

There's no question the White Sox were a great team with stars like Shoeless Joe Jackson, Buck Weaver, Hap Felsch, Chick Gandil, Eddie Cicotte, Lefty Williams, Eddie Collins, and Red Faber. But guess what? The Reds had their share of stars too; and, overshadowed by the Black Sox scandal, they were a team that gets very little notoriety.

In the featured photo above, we see the 1919 Reds team photo. Complete player identifications below.

The Reds were led by their great Hall-of Fame centerfielder, Edd Roush; and their roster included at least two other stars: Jack Daubert and Heine Groh. They were solid up and down their lineup, which included Ivey Wingo, Morrie Rath, Larry Kopf, and Greasy Neale.

With White Sox star Red Faber out for the series, the Reds actually had deeper pitching with starters Dutch Ruether, Hod Eller, Slim Sallee, Jimmy Ring, and Ray Fisher, plus relievers Dolf Luque and Rube Bressler, In a nine-game series, pitching depth was key. During the regular season, they had a significant advantage over the White Sox in team ERA: 2.23 to 3.04; plus they had 23 shutouts to the White Sox' 11.

While the White Sox had a higher team batting average (.287 to .263), the Reds had a better team fielding percentage (9.74 to 9.67), with 24 fewer errors during the regular season. They were managed by Pat Moran in his first season at the Reds' helm since taking over for the ailing Christy Mathewson. Moran had previously managed the Phillies (1915-

1918), going 323-257, and leading them to the 1915 National League pennant.

On February 1, the Reds obtained first baseman Jake Daubert from the Brooklyn Robins, releasing the notorious Hal Chase and thereby solidified their infield. In March, they added pitching depth as they signed Ray Fisher from the Yankees and Slim Sallee from the Giants off waivers.

The Reds were coming off a solid year (68-60) in the shortened 1918 season, and started 1919 with nine wins in the first ten games. After an 11-15 slump, they went 24-7 over their next 31 games. By late August they began to pull away from the league with an 81-34 record and a nine-game lead. They finished the season with a then franchise-best record of 96-44 and cruised to their first pennant since 1882 when the franchise was in the American Association.

Star centerfielder Edd Roush posted a league-leading .321 average, a team high 71 RBI, plus 20 stolen bases. Third baseman Heinie Groh hit .310 with a team-high five home runs, 63 RBI, and 21 stolen bases; while newly acquired Jake Daubert hit .276 with two home runs and 44 RBI. Outfielder Greasy Neale led the team with 28 stolen bases, while batting .242 with a home run and 54 RBI.

Hod Eller anchored the pitching staff, going 19-9 record with a 2.39 ERA, over 248 innings. Dutch Ruether led the National League with a .760 winning percentage (19-6), and a team-best 1.82 ERA. Slim Sallee led the Reds in victories with a 21-7 record, a 2.06 ERA and a team-high 22 complete games. Ray Fisher had a solid 14-5 record with a 2.17 ERA in 26 games.

It's interesting to read the reflections of the Reds' players on the 1919 World Series. Without exception, they all thought they had won fair and square. Some continued to believe that even after evidence to the contrary broke.[35]

Jake Daubert: "I was there, I saw them. We had the jump on the Sox in every game."

Larry Kopf: We didn't surmise a damn thing. I couldn't figure it out."

Ivy Wingo: "Cicotte worked hard to make us easy outs."

Hod Eller: "The White Sox were playing for keeps."

Greasy Neale: "There may have been some queer plays in Game One. But all the other games were honestly contested."

Edd Roush: "I can't yet see how they could play the way they did and throw the games. It's a mystery to me."

Heine Groh: "They seemed to be doing their level best to win. We attributed the stories to the White Sox not trying to 'sour grapes'. I didn't see anything that looked suspicious. But I think we'd have beaten them either way."

Reds' owner Garry Hermann: "...we believe firmly that we would have beaten them had every man of Comiskey's team played the string out and on the level." [36]

---

[35] All player quotes in this essay from *Burying the Black Sox*, pp. 22-24

[36] All Reds' players quotes from *Burying the Black Sox*, pp. 22-24

Overall this was a very solid Reds team. Were they as good as their 1970's descendants, the Big Red Machine? No, not by a long shot. But they were certainly no fluke; and, by the time the World Series rolled around, could very well have been the better team. Plus the White Sox were a faction-ridden team carrying extreme mental baggage; while the Reds were a close-knit group who, as the underdogs, played loose with nothing to lose.

1919 Cincinnati Reds Player Identifications

Top: Sherry Magee, Edd Roush, Morrie Rath, Hod Eller, Slim Sallee, Ed Garner, Ray Fisher. Middle: Jake Daubert, Charlie See, Dutch Ruether, Pat Moran, Bill Rariden, Nick Allen, Ivey Wingo, Greasy Neale. Front: Jimmy Smith, Dolf Luque, Pat Duncan, Larry Kopf, Ray Mitchell, Batboy.

# Was Charles Comiskey "Cheap"?

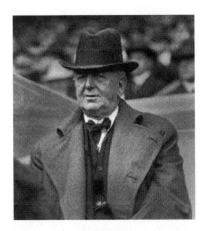

If you ask most knowledgeable baseball fans the question, "Why did eight Black Sox players conspired to 'fix' the 1919 World Series?" the answer you would likely hear is this: "It was Comiskey's fault. He was a cheapskate."

This reason for this response is not hard to uncover. The information most fans have about the 1919 World Series can be traced to Eliot Asinof's popular 1963 book, *Eight Men Out,* and the highly successful 1988 movie of the same name written and directed by John Sayles.

The "Comiskey was cheap" meme has been floating around baseball circles since the publication of *EMO*. It usually has two components: the first, the Old Roman allegedly ordered Eddie Cicotte benched toward the end of the season so that he could not earn a promised $10,000 bonus for winning 30 games; and the second, the White Sox of 1919 were grossly underpaid compared to the other major league teams.

Let's take a closer look at these two notions and see if they have validity.

Regarding the bonus, this passage from *Eight Men Out* is most likely where the story originated:

> There were betrayals too. Like Comiskey's promise to give Cicotte a $10,000 bonus in 1917 if he won thirty games. When the great pitcher threatened to reach that figure, it was said that Comiskey had him benched. The excuse, of course, was to rest him for the World Series.[37]

Did you catch that discrepancy? "…Comiskey's promise to give Cicotte a $10,000 bonus in 1917…" Did Asinof actually mean 1919? Was this just a typo that got past the editorial staff? In the movie, John Sayles moves the promise to the 1919 season; so the possibility of a typo is real. Anyway, that's how it appears in the book; so, until further notice, we'll have to consider the author meant 1917.

In addition, baseball researcher Rob Neyer has wondered where Asinof got this information about a bonus anyway – for either 1917 or 1919 - since there are no footnotes or sources in *EMO*. Did he just make it up? Neyer asks:

> "Asinof's source for this is unclear, and one begins by wondering how a story of this nature surfaces forty years after the fact."[38]

---

[37] *Burying the Black Sox*, p. 195
[38] Ibid, p. 194

One wonders, indeed...

When author Gene Carney interviewed Eliot Asinof while researching his own book, *Burying the Black Sox*, he actually got Asinof to admit that some of the stories and characters in *EMO* were fabrications; and also that many of his sources were, in his words, "amalgams of hundreds of conversation, impossible to document."[39] The problem is we don't know which ones are real and which ones are the fabrications. That's not exactly a ringing endorsement for the reliability of what many consider to be the "definitive book" on the Black Sox scandal.

The record actually shows that in both 1917 and 1919, Eddie had ample chances to win thirty games (he won 28 and 29 respectfully in those two seasons). There is no evidence that Comiskey prevented it from happening.

Looking at 1917 first, Gene Carney comments in *Burying the Black Sox*:

> The record shows that Cicotte started thirteen times in August and September 1917, with never more than five days between starts. A few times, he pitched on two days' rest, and also made four lengthy relief appearances. He had his chances to win thirty, all right, and he led the American League in innings pitched with 347, nineteen more than Walter Johnson.[40]

In addition, baseball researcher Neyer found no mention of a bonus in his search through *Chicago Tribune* archives. Eddie's salary since 1915 was

---

[39] *Burying the Black Sox*, p. 24
[40] Ibid, p. 194

$5,000 per season. So a promised bonus of $10,000 in 1917 seems farfetched, and even more unlikely in 1919, when salaries were depressed in the aftermath of World War I.

But what about 1919? After a strong August in which Eddie won four of six starts and two more in relief, Eddie slowed down in September. He won his first two starts and then had a two-week layoff. However, it was *Eddie* making the claim he had a sore arm, not the White Sox.

Eddie told friends that his arm "...was not lame, but very tired." But manager Gleason was quoted as saying Eddie's arm was fine, and he was expecting Eddie to be ready to pitch down the stretch:

> "Say, it always was all right and it's just the same now as it was. Those stories about Eddie having a sore arm were all wrong. He's ready for the Series."[41]

But the same day, it was Eddie being quoted in the *New York Times* as saying his arm had been lame a few week earlier in September. Again, researcher Bob Hoie has pointed out that this disagreement between Gleason and Cicotte is "exactly the opposite of what one would expect if Cicotte had been artificially held back from winning thirty games in order to cheat him out of a bonus."[42] The White Sox management wanted him pitching. Eddie was the one saying his arm was tired. And would the great knuckleballer have been saying this is a bonus of $10,000 was there waiting for him with just one more win? I think he'd be willing to pitch until his arm fell off.

---

[41] *The Chicago Tribune*, October 1, 1919
[42] *Burying the Black Sox*, p. 195

In recent years some hard evidence has turned up about Eddie's supposed bonus. His "transition card" has been found among 15,000 cards Major League Baseball donated to the National Baseball Hall of Fame in Cooperstown. These cards noted player movement from team to team, and also recorded each player's salary and other features of their contracts, like bonuses. Eddie's transition card has no mention of a bonus for winning 30 games in either 1917 or 1919.[43]

Many blame Comiskey for his low wages as the motive for the fix. They argue that if the players had been paid fair and decent salaries, they would not have been so willing to risk their careers for a $10,000 payout from the gamblers. But as far as the White Sox 1919 salaries are concerned, we learn this:

> Baseball researcher Bob Hoie argues that the 1919 White Sox might have had the top payroll in their league and perhaps in both leagues, around $90,000. In 1920, it was around 113,000. Hoie has been unable to find a team with a higher 1919 payroll.[44]

There's no doubt that Eddie Cicotte was underpaid in 1919. His salary should have been around $10,000, which is what he was paid in 1920. But the White Sox' overall payroll was possibly the highest in baseball. Resentment towards Comiskey could have spawned more from the knowledge that Eddie Collins was making $15,000. Was personal jealously a more likely motive?

So was Comiskey "cheap" and did that lead to the

---

[43] *Burying the Black Sox*, p. 197
[44] Ibid, p. 194

Black Sox scandal? Gene Carney comes to this conclusion:

> Comiskey's "Scrooge" image has spread thanks to *Eight Men Out,* and perhaps to the tendency to read into history assumptions about greedy players or tight- fisted owners. He was probably not exceptionally tight. Every owner wielded the reserve clause as the ultimate closer in contract negotiations. To think of Comiskey was the rule, and not the exception, is hard; but the facts seem to point in that direction. [45]

Comiskey's well-publicized treatment of the team may also have been a factor in the scheme to toss the Series, e.g., making them pay for their own laundry (or was this just another Asinof fabrication?). But it may well be that neither their salaries nor their working conditions were as strong a motive as the allure of making some "easy money" from the gamblers lurking around the sport. If you're looking for a motive, it might have been as simple as this: "Here's our chance to get back at that bastard Commy and make some real dough…"

Here's little history of Charles Comiskey's years in baseball:

Charles Comiskey was a key person in the formation of the American League, and was also the founding owner of the White Sox. He spent 49 years in baseball, as a player, manager, and owner. He broke into the game as a pitcher in 18892 with the St. Louis Browns of the American Association. Due to arm trouble, he shifted to first base and is credited with being the

---

[45] Ibid, p. 195

first to play hitters off the bag. Over his thirteen-year career, he hit .264, with 1530 RBI, 994 runs, and 416 stolen bases. As manager of the Browns from 1883-'89, he led them to four consecutive pennants (1885-'88), with an overall managerial record of 840-541 (.608). Under his ownership of the White Sox, the team won five pennants and two World Series championships (1906 and 1917).[46]

Charles Comiskey, "The Old Roman," passed away on October 26, 1931. Thousands of mourners from around the baseball world attended his funeral. He was inducted into the National Baseball Hall of Fame in 1939.

---

[46] Information from Charles Comiskey Wikipedia page

# White Sox Manager Kid Gleason

*"He was, without doubt, the gamest and most spirited ball player I ever saw and that doesn't except Ty Cobb. He was a great influence for good on any ball club, making up for his lack of stature by his spirit and fight. He could lick his weight in wildcats and would prove it at the drop of a hat."*- John McGraw[47]

"The 1919 White Sox are the best team in the world, they have no weaknesses!" –Manager Kid Gleason

There was a lot more to Kid Gleason's career than just the Black Sox Scandal. He was a scrappy, gutsy little ballplayer who started out as a pitcher and later became the starting second baseman for one of the greatest teams in baseball history, the famous Baltimore Orioles of the 1890s. Always an asset to any team he was associated with, by the time of his death in 1933, he was one of the most beloved figures in the game.

The Camden, New Jersey native acquired the nickname "Kid" early in life because of his short

---

[47] Quotes in this essay from SABR biography of Kid Gleason, by Dan Lindner: https://sabr.org/bioproj/person/632ed912

stature (5'7", 160 pounds as an adult), and his youthful, spirited nature. Over his long, 22-year major league career (1888-1908, 1912), he played for the Phillies, Browns, Orioles, Giants, and White Sox.

In eight seasons as a pitcher, Kid went 138-131 with a 3.79 ERA. Amidst the turmoil caused by the Players League competition in 1890, Kid compiled an unbelievable season: 38-17 (.691), over 506 innings, 2.63 ERA, and 51 complete games. To show what a crazy year it was in baseball, none of these statistics even led the National League. Bill Hutchinson pitched 603 innings that year for Chicago!

His career batting average was a respectable .261 with 1946 hits, 216 doubles, 81 triples, and 824 RBIs. In Kid's two years with the Orioles (1894 and '95), he hit a combined .371 with a .404 on-base percentage, as the Orioles won their first two of three straight National League pennants. A true baseball "lifer," he's one of the small group of players who have appeared in the major leagues in four decades.

In the featured photo above, we can see that the cares and stresses of the 1919 World Series scandal are deeply woven into the face of Kid Gleason.

After his playing career ended, Gleason became a coach with the White Sox. He was named manager on December 31, 1918, succeeding Pants Rowland. In his first season as manager, Kid led the White Sox to the 1919 pennant with a record of 88-52, but lost to the Cincinnati Reds in the ill-fated 1919 World Series, amidst allegations that the Series had been thrown.

The 1919 White Sox were quite a team, with a roster

stacked with star players up and down the lineup, including stars Shoeless Joe Jackson, Buck Weaver, Eddie Cicotte, Eddie Collins, Ray Schalk, and Red Faber, the latter three Hall-of-Famers. Acquiring the personality of their manager, they played with the same spark and determination Kid showed during his career, leading the league in runs, batting average, and stolen bases. As is well documented, the scandal resulted in lifetime bans for eight White Sox players. Gleason was not involved, and some historians have noted that he was among those who alerted White Sox owner Charles Comiskey of the fix.

Author Gene Carney, in his acclaimed book, *Burying the Black Sox*, uncovered evidence that Gleason, aware of the rumors about a fix circulating at the start of the Series, confronted the team. He later told a reporter, "Something was wrong. I didn't like the betting odds." Carney added that Gleason said little about the fix for the record later, but that his communication to his team, especially his ace pitchers, may have resulted in the fix being called off right after his confrontation.

The White Sox were in a close pennant race again in 1920, but fell out after the eight suspensions came down with three games left in the season. With a roster depleted of its stars, the White Sox went a dismal 208-254 over his last three years at the helm. He finished his managerial career with a 392-364 record.

Kid was out of baseball for two years, but the allure of returning to the game proved to be too much to resist. Connie Mack gave him an opportunity to return to the coaching ranks with the Athletics. Kid was aboard for two World Series championships with the Athletics in 1929 and 1930 and a third pennant in 1931.

Suffering from a heart ailment, Gleason retired after the 1931 season and eventually became bedridden about the time of the 1932 World Series. He passed away on January 2, 1933. Understandably, Kid was said to be personally affected by the Black Sox scandal for the rest of his life, which may have contributed to his early demise at age 66.

That Kid Gleason was one of the most beloved figures in the game was apparent at his funeral, attended by an estimated 5,000 people, including such baseball notables as John McGraw, Connie Mack, and Commissioner Landis.

Let's take a moment to remember a great baseball "lifer," Kid Gleason, who, because of the 1919 Black Sox scandal, became one of the game's most tragic figures.

# Reds Manager Pat Moran

Ninety-five years ago on this date, baseball "lifer" Pat Moran passed away while at Spring Training with the Reds in Orlando, Florida. That was sad to read, but what I found really surprising was that Moran was only 48. If you're like me, I bet you thought he was a lot older. He certainly looked it in all the old pictures I've seen of him. I would have guessed he was in his 60's, at least.

Pat Moran played 14 seasons in the major leagues for the Boston Bean Eaters (1901-05), Cubs (1906-09), and Phillies (1910-14). While there's not a lot to say about his lack-luster career (.262, 17 home runs, 262 RBIs), Pat left his mark on the game as a manager. He posted a 748-586 mark (.561) over nine seasons, winning first-ever National League pennants for the Phillies (1915) and Reds (1919).

Moran spent most of his career as a back-up catcher. He utilized his time on the "pines" wisely, and became a student of the game. He specialized in the mental aspects of pitching, trying to understand what made some pitchers successful, while others, with equal amounts of talent, failed. As a player-coach with the Phillies in 1913-1914, he took a young right-hander named Grover Cleveland "Pete" Alexander under his wing. With Pat's wise counsel and guidance,

Alexander developed into one of the greatest pitchers in the history of the game.

Moran retired as a player after the 1914 season, but by then his obvious leadership qualities were noticed by Phillies' front office, and he was immediately promoted to manager. After a sixth place finish in 1914 due to defections (and threatened defections) to the Federal League, Moran's 1915 Phillies— led by Alexander's 31 wins and Gavvy Cravath's slugging—improved by 17 games and won their first National League pennant. They lost the 1915 World Series four games to one to the Red Sox. The Phillies finished second in both 1916 and 1917. With baseball disrupted by World War I – and with the trade of Pete Alexander to the Cubs – the Phillies sank below .500 in 1918 and Moran was fired.

Pat was not unemployed for long, as he was hired to succeed the ailing Christy Mathewson as Reds manager for the 1919 season. The Reds had finished third, 15½ games behind in 1918, but under Moran they showed immediate improvement, taking the 1919 National League pennant by nine games. They then defeated the White Sox in the 1919 World Series five games to three to win Cincinnati's first championship.

This should have been Moran's crowning accomplishment. But when it was charged that eight key members of the White Sox had conspired with gamblers to "throw" the series, the Reds' achievement appeared tainted. After the scandal broke, Moran and his players and many baseball experts furiously argued—with some merit—that the great Reds team would have won the Series under any circumstances.

The Reds fell to third in 1920, and then to sixth in 1921, followed by two second place finishes in 1922 and '23. While spending the winter of 1923-24 at his Fitchburg, MA. home, Moran was taken ill. He was able to report to the Reds' training camp in Orlando, Florida, but his condition worsened and he died there at the age of 48. The cause of death was listed as Bright's disease, a kidney ailment, but some baseball historians ascribe Moran's fatal illness to alcoholism.

# Kenesaw Mountain Landis: Commissioner or Czar, Hero or Villain?

By Bill Gutman

*"We want a man as chairman who will rule with an iron hand. Baseball has lacked a hand like that for years. It needs it now worse than ever. Therefore, it is our object to appoint a big man to lead the new commission."* – National League President John Heydler on the search for the first baseball commissioner.[48]

He was major league baseball's first commissioner. Unlike his successors, he wasn't an employee of the owners. He demanded and received full autonomy before taking the job. As a federal judge he was used to being the boss, giving the orders. He would accept no less from the men looking to hire someone to clean up the national pastime following the high-profile Black Sox scandal of 1919. Kenesaw Mountain Landis certainly made his mark on baseball. But was he a hero or villain? Did he benefit baseball or harm it, or was he somewhere in between? Let's take a

---

[48] National Baseball Hall of Fame on-line: https://baseballhall.org/hall-of-famers/landis-kenesaw

look at his Hall of Fame legacy.

Landis was both a strange and dynamic character. He was thin to the point of almost being frail, with a shock of often unkempt white hair. When he was named commissioner in November of 1920, he looked older than his 54 years. He had a reputation for theatrics in his courtroom after being named a judge of the U.S. District Court of Northern Illinois by President Theodore Roosevelt in 1905.

Born on November 20, 1866, in Millville, Ohio, his military surgeon father decided to name him after the Civil War Battle of Kennesaw Mountain. The name didn't please his family and Abraham Landis left an "n" out of Kennesaw, but it was certainly a name people would remember. By 1920, Judge Landis had a reputation as a moralist and prohibitionist, someone who railed against the evils of drinking and gambling. Yet friends said he could swear like a sailor when the mood struck him.

The lords of major league baseball took a fancy to the judge in 1915 when the rival Federal League brought the major leagues to court in an antitrust action. Landis stonewalled his decision for some 11 months until league officials, tired of waiting, began selling off the teams and the league disbanded. For his non-decision, Judge Landis was front and center when the Black Sox scandal broke. His name was the first mentioned when the idea of naming a Commissioner of Baseball was discussed. After all, he was a man known for his integrity, as well as being a fan of the game who loved the Chicago Cubs.

Kenesaw Mountain Landis was formally offered the job on November 12, 1920, a year after word of the fix in the 1919 World Series became baseball's hottest topic. He took the job only after the owners granted him the absolute power over the game that he demanded. Many felt at the time that the Black Sox scandal brought the problem of gambling and gamblers infiltrating the game to the fore. Shenanigans involving gambling were fairly common up to that time. The owners often let it slide due to fear of hurting the game.

An example had to be made, and after the eight named players on the White Sox were acquitted in a jury trial, Landis made his first statement as commissioner, one he knew had to be strong and decisive. He said:

"Regardless of the verdict of juries, no player that sits in a conference with a bunch of crooked players and gamblers where the ways and means of throwing games are discussed, and does not promptly tell his club about it, will ever again play professional baseball."

So the eight, including the great Shoeless Joe Jackson and Buck Weaver, both of whom had excelled in the 1919 World Series, were gone with Landis adamant they'd never be reinstated. "There is absolutely no chance for any of them to creep back into organized baseball," he said. "They will be and remain outlaws." During the rest of his tenure, Landis opposed any efforts to reinstate the banned players. They weren't alone. In his first decade as commissioner he would banish 11 players for gambling-related offenses. His actions certainly cut down on player involvement with gamblers.

Was the Black Sox scandal the highlight of Judge

Landis' tenure as commissioner? Let's take a look at some of his other decisions or non-decisions. There was a rule in place, perhaps an outdated one that prohibited players from barnstorming after the season. The player who openly defied it was non-other-than Babe Ruth, the game's greatest attraction. When told that Landis prohibited him from barnstorming, the defiant Babe suggested the commissioner "go jump in a lake." The result was that both the Babe and teammate Bob Meusel were suspended for the first 40 games of the 1922 season.

When two of the game's greatest stars, Ty Cobb and Tris Speaker, were accused by retired pitcher Dutch Leonard of conspiring with him (Cobb's Detroit teammate) and Smoky Joe Wood (Speaker's teammate with Cleveland), to throw a game between the teams back in 1919, Landis took no action. Leonard supposedly had letters to back up his claims, but Landis ruled that Leonard was driven by a personal grudge. Wood was retired, but Cobb and Speaker were allowed to finish out their careers.

In 1930, Landis noted that the growth of farm systems were allowing owners to stockpile players, often keeping major league worthy players in the minors. He made a test case of outfielder Fred Bennett, who was in the St. Louis Browns system, and declared him a free agent. Browns' owner Phil Ball took the commissioner to federal court and lost. It's said that by the end of the 1930s Landis had freed nearly 200 minor league players. The owners, obviously, weren't happy.

In 1943, Landis again showed his aversion to gambling by banishing Phillies' owner William Cox for life for betting on games. But that was part of a chain of events that ultimately put a shameful mark on Judge Landis tenure. A year earlier, Bill Veeck, Jr. wanted to buy the Phillies from then-owner Gary Nugent. He made it no secret that he wanted to fill his wartime roster with players in the Negro Leagues and apparently told Judge Landis of his plan. A day later the National League took control of the team, and, with Landis' approval, sold it to William Cox. Landis had often said that baseball had no written rule to prevent African-Americans from playing, but here and in other instances he made no effort to eliminate the unwritten rule. No African-American played in the big leagues while he was commissioner.

But everything wasn't rosy. By 1944, many of the owners wanted Landis out. Many referred to him as a czar, while the press and public continued to support him. That fall, with his health failing, the owners gave Landis a new seven-year contract. But they did it with the knowledge that he might not last much longer, and they were right. Eight days after getting his new contract, Kenesaw Mountain Landis died at the age of 78.

New York sportswriter Tom Meany hit the nail on the head when he wrote, shortly before Landis' death, that if the commissioner were ousted the man who replaced him would "merely be an employee. And who ever heard of any employee finding against his bosses." That's exactly what happened and continues that way today.

You can take the good with the bad, but one thing is certain. There will never be a baseball commissioner quite like Kenesaw Mountain Landis. He was one of a kind.

# EDDIE COLLINS: "CLEAN SOX" AND ALL-TIME GREAT

## By Bill Gutman

As the 100th anniversary of the Black Sox scandal in the 1919 World Series draws nearer, we will be turning our attention—in addition of the "Eight Men Out"— to other members of the team, including the three Hall-of-Famers, manager Kid Gleason, and other players of note.

Today, Bill Gutman starts us off with an interesting article on Hall-of-Fame second baseman Eddie Collins. I think you'll find it interesting to discover what a great all-around player Eddie was, one of the best ever:

*I put on a uniform that did not fit me too well. Gosh, I weighed only about 140 pounds. I was self-conscious among all those big fellows—men like Rube Waddell —whom I had read so much about.* – Eddie Collins, on his first game as a major leaguer [49]

Eddie Collins always played the game the right way. It was team first and he always used his considerable tools to help them win. In the Dead Ball Era he often bunted, sacrificed runners, stole a base—a lot of

---

[49] SABR biography of Eddie Collins, by Paul Mittermeyer: https://sabr.org/bioproj/person/c480756d

them—was a great hit-and-run man, and slapped hits all over the field. When the so-called lively ball was introduced in 1920 he didn't miss a beat taking what the pitchers gave him and had a career best 224 hits and hit a career high .372. When his 25-year career ended in 1930 he had 3,315 hits (11th all-time), a .333 lifetime average (26th all-time), 741 stolen bases (eighth all-time), and a lifetime on-base percentage of .424 (12th all-time). He also holds the all-time career record for sacrifice hits with 512. It's no wonder he was elected to the Hall of Fame in 1939.

Today, however, many remember Eddie Collins for something else. He was a member of the 1919 Chicago White Sox, the infamous team said to have thrown the World Series that year and a team now forever known as the Black Sox. Collins, however, was never implicated in the fix in any way. He was one of the so-called "Clean" Sox, a bright, college educated player at the time when few major leaguers attended college, and thus was often unpopular among many of his less sophisticated teammates.

Eddie Collins was born on May 2, 1887, in Millerton, New York, though his family moved to Tarrytown, New York, before Eddie reached his first birthday. He excelled in school as he grew up and, despite his small stature, also played football and baseball. In the fall of 1903, at the tender age of 16, he enrolled at Columbia University and become a 135-pound quarterback on the freshman football team. In the spring he became the starting shortstop on the school's baseball team. "At that time I liked football better than baseball," he would say.

But by 1906 he was playing semi-pro baseball

for several area teams when a pitcher for the Philadelphia A's spotted him and told his boss, Connie Mack, about the 19-year-old infielder. After getting a full scouting report, Mack signed him to a contract. He got his feet wet playing in six games for the A's at the end of the 1906 season and then 14 more the next year. By 1908 he was good enough to play 102 games for Mack and the A's, hitting a respectable .273. A year later he became a starter and really showed what he could do.

In 1909, Eddie played in 153 games, becoming ensconced as the A's second baseman. He batted .347 that year with 198 hits and 63 stolen bases. He also led all second basemen in assists, put outs, double plays and fielding percentage. No way they were about to get him off the field. Starting in 1910, Connie Mack's A's won four pennants and three world championships in five years. The team was spearheaded by what was called the "$100,000 Infield," the name given more for their ability than their salaries. It featured Frank "Home Run" Baker at third, Jack Barry at short, Eddie at second and Stuffy McInnis at first.

Eddie excelled during this time, stealing a league-leading 81 bases in 1910 and sporting batting averages of .324, .365, .348, .345 and .344 over that five-year period. Though a star, some teammates saw him as cocky, even giving him that as a nickname. But there was little doubt he was an extremely smart player, adept at reading pitchers when stealing bases, rarely slumping at the plate, and fielding brilliantly. In 1914, he won a Chalmers automobile as the league's Most Valuable Player. Today they would call him a superstar.

Oddly enough, due to inroads made by the Federal League, which was raiding players, Mack decided to break up his team; and, in December, sold Eddie to the White Sox for $50,000. Charles Comiskey agreed to pay him $15,000, plus a $10,000 signing bonus. He immediately became Chicago's highest paid player. During the 1915 season the White Sox also acquired Shoeless Joe Jackson and were en route to becoming the best team in the league. By 1917 they won 100 games and the pennant before beating John McGraw's Giants in the World Series. Eddie was a champion once more.

The Sox were a divided team. Many of the players, led by Chick Gandil, didn't like Eddie. Once again it was that he was different, educated and more sophisticated. By 1919 things were coming to a boil. Eddie described it this way:

"[The club] was torn by discord and hatred during much of the '19 season. From the moment I arrived at training camp . . . I could see that something was amiss. We may have had our troubles in other years, but in 1919 we were a club that pulled apart rather than together. There were frequent arguments and open hostility. All the things you think—and are taught to believe—are vital to the success of any athletic organization were missing from it, and yet it was the greatest collection of players ever assembled, I would say."

That statement alone could explain how the Black Sox Scandal happened without going into the details. Enough said. Eddie stayed with the Sox until 1926, still hitting .344 at the age of 39. He played the last four years back in Philadelphia, but saw very little action the final three. After his retirement he coached for the A's for a couple of years, then joined the Boston Red Sox as vice president and general manager. He remained with the Bosox the rest of his working life, taking a notable scouting trip to California in which he signed two future Hall of Famers, Bobby Doerr and the one and only Ted Williams.

Ill health finally forced him to relinquish his General Manager duties after 1947, though he was still a vice president. A cerebral hemorrhage in August of 1950 debilitated him and his heart finally gave out on March 23, 1951. He was just 63 years old.

John McGraw once called him "the best ballplayer I have seen in my career on the diamond," and Bill James, the baseball historian and analyst, working a "win shares" statistical rating system, ranked Eddie Collins as the greatest second baseman of all time. Once again, enough said.

# EDD ROUSH – ONE TOUGH HALL OF FAMER

## By Bill Gutman

*"I've played against him for years and I played with him one year. You guys get back on the bench and quit throwing at this guy. He'll take us all out of here."* – Rogers Hornsby speaking about Edd Roush [50]

Edd Roush hated pitchers throwing at him. Whenever they did he'd take it out on the nearest defender, usually with his spikes. He also hated it when he felt owners were short-changing him and was willing to hold out at a time when the owners held all the trump cards. On top of that, he hated spring training. He felt he stayed in shape working his farm and hunting around his home in Oakland City, Indiana. There was little doubt that Edd Roush did it his way, and did it exceedingly well. Not only was he a magician with the bat, but he was also considered the best outfielder in the National League during the Dead Ball Era and beyond.

Roush played in the majors for 18 seasons, from 1913

---

[50] SABR biography of Edd Roush by Jim Sandoval: https://sabr.org/bioproj/person/26fd7901

to 1931, including two in the Federal League, despite sitting out the 1930 season in a salary dispute. His major league career began with the White Sox for a year, then two in the Federal League, and part of a season with the Giants before spending the bulk of his time with Cincinnati. He was called the perfect Dead Ball Era hitter, winning batting titles in both 1917 and 1919, yet he had his best batting averages once the lively ball came into play in 1920. Between 1920 and 1925 Roush hit .339, .352, .352, .351, .348 and .339. How's that for consistency? And he did it in his own, unique way

The 5'11", 170-pound Roush was a southpaw swinger who used a short, but thick-handled bat that weighed a hefty 48 ounces. It was one of the heaviest bats in the game at that time. He credited his strong arms and wrists, which he said came from doing hard work around his family's farm, for his ability to handle the heavy piece of lumber. And he did it the Wee Willie Keeler way, hitting line drives all over the field and often between the fielders. It was place-hitting par excellence.

"Place hitting is, in a sense, glorified bunting," he once said. "I only take a half swing at the ball, and the weight of the bat rather than my swing is what drives it." He was quick enough to shift his feet after the ball left the pitcher's hand and would gauge the timing of his swing to where he wanted to hit the ball. A quick snap of the bat was all it took to finish the job and he finished it to the tune of 2,376 career hits.

That wasn't all Edd Roush could do. He was also one of the best centerfielders in the game, often compared with the American League's Tris Speaker. The speedy Roush had the ability to turn his back after the ball was hit and run to spot where it would come down, most times in his glove. He also had a powerful throwing arm, and while he always threw left-handed he had the ability to throw with his right arm, as well. He once played 10 games at second base in the minors and made all his throws right-handed. Of his outfield play, Cincy teammate Heinie Groh once said, "Eddie used to take care of the whole outfield, not just center. He was far and away the best outfielder I ever saw."

Edd Roush was born on May 8, 1893, in Oakland City. He had a twin brother, Fred, who also played ball but never made it to the majors. In 1909 Edd was playing semi-pro ball with a local team, the Oakland City Walkovers. By 1913 he was with Evansville in the Kitty League when in August, his contract was sold to the White Sox. He jumped his contract the next season and went to Indianapolis of the Federal League, hitting .325 in a championship season. The team moved to Newark in 1916 and when the league folded, the New York Giants bought his contract.

He played just 39 games for the Giants and hated it, not approving of the methods used by manager John McGraw. "If you made a bad play he'd cuss you out, yell at you, call you all sorts of names," Edd said. "That didn't go with me."

In July, he was traded to Cincinnati a deal that included the great Christy Mathewson, who would become the Reds' manager. In Cincy, Edd found a home and really began his Hall of Fame career in earnest. It began when Mathewson made Edd his centerfielder, a position for which he was perfectly suited.

By 1919, Edd began his practice of holding out for more money and he would conveniently miss most or all of spring training, which he always felt was unnecessary, at least for him. That year he helped lead the Reds to the National League pennant, with his league-best .321 batting average, a season in which he also had 19 triples. That, of course, was also the year of the Black Sox Scandal in which the Reds topped the White Sox, five games to three in a best of nine Series. Edd hit just .214 in the Fall Classic, but his six hits resulted in seven RBIs.

As for the Sox "throwing" the Series, Edd would state for the rest of his life that he felt the Reds were the better team. He was often quoted as saying that after the first two games the White Sox played to win because the gamblers had not paid them off properly. He obviously acknowledged that there was hanky-panky going on. He also told a story that Reds pitcher "Hod" Eller was approached by a gambler before the eighth and final game and was offered $5000 in cash to throw the game. Eller confirmed the story saying he told the man if he didn't get out of his way he'd punch him square in the nose.

Ironically, after the 1926 season, he was traded back to McGraw's Giants at a time when age was beginning to catch up with him. McGraw told him, "I've been trying to get you back ever since I traded you a long time ago. Now you're either going to play for me or you're not going to play at all." Once again Edd held out and finally agreed to a three-year contract worth $70,000, something almost unheard of back then. He played for the Giants for three seasons, missing a good part of 1928 when he needed surgery to repair torn stomach muscles. In 1930 he sat out the entire year, again over a contract dispute, then returned to

Cincinnati for a final season in 1931. He retired with a .323 lifetime batting average and great numbers across the board.

Retirement was good to him. He was smart with his money and made some solid investments. He built a house in Bradenton, Florida, where he spent the winters. He was inducted into both the Indiana and Ohio Baseball Halls of Fame, and in 1960 to the Cincinnati Reds Hall of Fame. The ultimate honor came two years later when he went to Cooperstown, inducted along with Jackie Robinson, Bob Feller and his longtime friend, Bill McKechnie. In 1969's baseball centennial celebration, Edd Roush was named the greatest player in Cincinnati Reds history.

The player that Reds' manager Pat Moran once called "the great individualist in the game" died on March 21, 1988, at the ripe old age of 94.

# Another Look at the Black Sox Scandal: Other Notable White Sox Players

As I near the end of my series of essays on the 1919 World Series, I'd like to say a few words about some of the other players on the two teams besides the "Eight Men Out."[51]

We've already highlighted the careers of the great Hall-of-Fame stars Eddie Collins and Edd Roush; plus managers Kid Gleason and Pat Moran. But there were a few other notable players on both team who often get overlooked by the scandal that shook the baseball world to its core in 1919.

Today we'll shine the spotlight on White Sox players. In the next post, we'll take a look a notable Reds.

In the great featured photo, we see members of the 1917 World Series Champion White Sox, all of whom were on the 1919 team: Joe Jackson, Shano Collins, Hap Felsch, Eddie Murphy, Nemo Leibold.

---

[51] Statistical information on White Sox players from Baseball Reference.com

# 1919 White Sox

**Ray "Cracker" Schalk**: In an 18-year career all with the White Sox, the 5'6" Ray Schalk played in 1760 games with a career batting average of .253 and 1,345 hits. He was known as the greatest defensive catcher of his era and an excellent handlers of pitchers. He retired with a career fielding average of .981. Schalk was said to have revolutionized the way the catching position was played, with the addition of speed and defensive. He managed the White Sox for one season (1927); and was elected to the Hall of Fame in 1956. He is the only catcher in major league history to catch for a father-son combination: "Big Ed" Walsh and his son, Ed Walsh, Jr.

**John "Shano" Collins:** In a 16-year career, Shano Collins hit .264 with 1,687 hits. He was the first batter of the 1919 World Series, leading off Game One, and hit .250 in the four games in which he appeared. His best year was 1920 when he hit .303. Before the 1921 season, he was traded to the Red Sox and played for them through the 1925 season. He later managed the Red Sox (1931-32). Collins still holds the major league career record of eight triples with the bases loaded. In ten World Series games, all with the White Sox, he hit .270 (10-37) with four runs scored.

**Urban "Red" Faber**: One of the White Sox all-time great pitchers, Red missed the 1919 World Series due to illness, but went 23-13 in 1920. He was a spitball pitcher and was one of 18 pitchers allowed to continue throwing the "wet one" after the ban in 1920. He played 20 years in the majors, all with the White Sox, and had a career record of 254-213 with a 3.15 ERA. He had the 17th-highest victory total in history at the time of his retirement and was elected to the Hall of fame in 1964. Red was one of only six pitchers to win 100 or more games in both the "dead ball" (through 1920) and live ball eras.

**Dickie Kerr**: Dickie pitched four seasons in the majors, going 53-34 with an ERA of 3.84. He won two games in the 1919 World Series, posting a combined 1.42 ERA. His best season was 1920 when he went 21-9 for the White Sox. After his playing career, he was a minor league manager and scout, and is credited with converting a young pitcher named Stan Musial into an outfielder. Musial was so grateful that he named his first son, "Richard" after Dickie Kerr.

**Harry "Nemo" Leibold**: Nemo played 13 years in the majors, hitting .266 with 1,109 hits. His single in the ninth inning of the1917 White Sox **drove in** Buck Weaver with the final run of the championship-clinching game for the White Sox. Prior to the 1921 season, he was traded, along with Shano Collins, to the Red Sox for Harry Hooper. He was the last surviving member of the 1917 and 1919 pennant-winning White Sox. The 5'6" Leibold was one of only three regulars not accused of involvement in the Black Sox scandal. His best season was 1920 when he hit .306 with 143 hits. Nemo saw World Series action with the Senators in 1924 and '25 as a teammate of the great Walter Johnson.

**Erskine Mayer**: Mayer played eight seasons in the majors, with a 91-70 record and 2.96 ERA. His career ended with the 1919 World Series. He had been purchased off waivers by the White Sox in August of 1919 to add veteran help to the stretch drive. Mayer had been a member of the 1915 pennant-winning Phillies, pitching the second game of the World Series that year against the Red Sox, going nine innings in a 2-1 loss. One of our readers, John Mayer, is a family descendant of Erskine Mayer.

**"Clean Eddie" Murphy**: Over his 11-year career in the majors, Eddie hit .287 with 680 hits. He had his best season in 1920, hitting .339 with 40 hits in 118 at-bats, primarily as a pinch hitter. In addition to 1919, he had played in the 1912 and 1914 World Series as a member of the Philadelphia A's.

# Another Look at the Black Sox Scandal: Other Notable Reds Players

As I near the end of my essays on the 1919 World Series, I'd like to say a few words about some of the other players on the two teams besides the "Eight Men Out."[52]

We've already highlighted the careers of the great Hall-of-Fame stars Eddie Collins and Edd Roush; plus managers Kid Gleason and Pat Moran. But there were other notable players on both teams who often get overlooked by the scandal that shook the baseball world to its core in 1919.

Today we'll shine the spotlight on Reds players.

## 1919 Reds

**Jake Daubert:** In a 15-year career that many think is Hall-of-Fame worthy, Daubert hit .303, with 2326 hits, two National League batting titles, and the 1914 Chalmers Most Valuable Player Award.

---

[52] Statistical information on Reds players from Baseball Reference.com

**Hod Eller**: Hod was the ace of the Reds staff in 1919, going 20-9, then tailed off to 13-12 in 1920. He spent his entire five-year career with the Reds, retiring after the 1921 season with a record of 61-40.

**Ray Fisher:** Ray came to the Reds on waivers following the1918 season with the U.S. Army. He retired after a 10-year career in the majors in 1920, with a record of100-94 and a 2.82 ERA. After the 1920 season, he requested a release from the Reds rather than accept a $1,000 pay cut. For this reason, he was banned by Judge Landis for life. He then accepted a position as baseball and freshman football coach at the University of Michigan and stayed there for 38 years, winning nine Big Ten baseball titles. One of the football players he coached was future-president, Gerald Ford. In 1980, Commissioner Bowie Kuhn reinstated Fisher as a player in good standing.

**Heinie Groh**: Famous for his bottle bat, Heine played 16 seasons in the majors, with a career .292 batting average and 1,774 hits. He followed 1919 hitting .298 in 1920, and .331 in 1921. Traded to the Giants after the 1921 season, Heine hit .474 in the 1922 World Series. He also made an appearance in the 1927 World Series with the Pirates. Following his playing days, he remained in baseball as a scout and minor league manager.

**Dolf Luque**: Known as the "Pride of Cuba," he was one of the first native Cubans to star in the major leagues. Over his 20-year career, he went 194-179, with a 3.24 ERA, and 206 complete games over 3,220 innings. He had a truly amazing season in 1922, with a 27-8 record, leading the National League in wins (27), winning percentage (.771), ERA (1.93), and shutouts (16). He made an appearance in the 1933 World Series with the Giants at the age of 43. Following retirement, he remained in the game as a coach.

**Sherry Magee**: His brilliant 16-year career came to an end after the 1919 World Series. Playing in 2085 games, he batted .291 with 2,169 hits. He had led the National League in hitting in 1910 (.331), and in RBIs in 1910 and 1915. After his playing days, he umpired for one year in the National League.

**Earle "Greasy" Neale**: Greasy had a great World Series in 1919, as the Reds leading hitter at .357 and 13 total bases. Over his eight-year career, he hit .259. Known for his speed, he had 139 stolen bases. During the off season, Greasy played football and coached at the college level. After his baseball career ended, he turned full-time to football, and in 1940 was hired as coach of the Philadelphia Eagles. Under his leadership, the Eagles won the 1948 and 1949 NFL titles and appeared in three straight NFL championship games. He was elected to the Pro Football Hall of Fame.

**Bill Rariden**: Bill wrapped up a 12-year major league career in 1920 with a .237 career average. He was part of one of the most famous World Series plays. He was the Giants' catcher in the decisive sixth game of the 1917 World Series as Eddie Collins broke for home on a tapper back to the mound. Rariden moved up the third base line, leaving home plate unprotected, as Eddie Collins raced home ahead of the chasing Heine Zimmerman in hot pursuit.

**Morrie Rath**: The Reds first batter in the 191 World Series, he was plunked by Eddie Cicotte in what was apparently a signal to the gamblers that the fix was on. He played six years in the majors hitting .264. He was one of only four players to play in a triple header in the modern era, which he did on the last day of his career, October 2, 1920. He served in the U.S. Navy in World War I.

**Dutch Ruether**: Dutch played 11 seasons in the majors, going 137-95 with a 3.50 ERA. An excellent hitter, he batted .667 in the 1919 World Series and .351 over the 1920 season. He also appeared in the 1926 World Series with the Yankees.

**Slim Salle**: Slim played 14 seasons in the majors, going 173-143 with a 2.36 ERA. He got his nickname by carrying 180 pounds on his 6'3" frame. He retired after the 1921 season while with the Giants. He won Game Two of the 1919 World Series, getting some revenge against the White Sox, as they had beaten him twice in the 1917 World Series.

# Another Look At the 1919 World Series: The Eye-Witness Accounts

I've always found it interesting that many of the eyewitnesses to the 1919 World Series apparently saw something completely different than what has become accepted as the conventional wisdom.[53]

To me, it just doesn't all add up...

While there can be no doubt that the "Eight Men Out" conspired with gamblers and dirty money was given and accepted, do we know for certain that the Series was actually "thrown"? Some games? All games? None of us was there; so we have to rely on the recorded contemporary testimony of those who were. And many contemporary accounts paint a totally different picture. Can it be possible that there's more to the story than meets the eye?

Official Scorer James C. Hamilton testified that he only saw one possible suspicious play in the entire Series (the Cicotte deflection in Game Four, which I'll cover in another post).[54] National League umpire

---

[53] All quotes in this essay from Burying the Black Sox, except where indicated
[54] Burying the Black Sox, p. 172

Richard Nallin had "no suspicion whatever of any wrong-doing." American League Umpire Billy Evans, a future Hall-of-Famer, likewise said, "Well, I guess I'm just a big dope. That series looked all right to me."

Umpire Ernie Quigley was quoted as saying: "...I never saw a team try harder to win and they were beaten on the square by the superior strength of the Reds." Quigley also mentioned two great plays by Roush and Morrie Rath: *"But for these two plays the White Sox would have won at least two more games, which would have meant the series for them."*[55]

Hmmm...Shouldn't that last statement alone start us thinking? How does the "conventional wisdom" account for that?

The Reds players, including Roush, Groh, Greasy Neale, Dutch Ruether, Hod Eller, Slim Sallee, Dolf Luque, Jake Daubert, Larry Kopf, Ivy Wingo, and owner Garry Hermann thought the Series was played on the level. Roush always remained doubtful that the Series was fixed and maintained the best team had won.

Reds manager Pat Moran was also skeptical: "If they threw some of the games they must be consummate actors, and their place is on the stage, for nothing in their playing gave us the impression they weren't doing their best....It is astonishing to me that [they] could get away with that sort of thing and us not know it."

Even "Clean Sox" Ray Schalk said that "Jackson and Cicotte gave their best all the way;" and Eddie Collins claimed he was "never suspicious of their

---

[55] The Sporting News, October 7, 1920

actions during the Series." Christy Mathewson, sitting with Hugh Fullerton looking for suspicious play, concluded it would be impossible to throw a World Series.

Many of the sportswriters reached the same conclusion, including *Sporting News* and *Baseball Magazine* reporters. W.A. Phelan wrote that "… if ever a Series was played upon the level, this was one," adding, "The Reds simply outclassed the overconfident White Sox." Henry P. Edwards concurred: "[the notion that] the Sox were guilty of intentional bad play is something that cannot be swallowed," as did James O'Leary: "If anybody was 'fixed' give us his name and the evidence showing that he was fixed, and who fixed him."

Could all these eye-witnesses all have been fooled? These were not casual fans, but baseball lifers. And what about the many outstanding plays made by Jackson, Weaver, and Felsch; and the clutch hits by, of all players, Gandil? But for a few spectacular plays, most notably by the great center fielder Edd Roush, the entire Series may have had a different result.

One hundred years later, is it still necessary for us to blindly accept the "conventional wisdom" without questioning it? Is it possible that the Black Sox - while certainly guilty of conspiring with gamblers and taking dirty money – didn't really know what they had gotten themselves into by the time the Series started and didn't know what to do? In light of the eyewitness testimony, isn't that a question worthy of investigation?

This is not to exonerate the Black Sox by any

means. It's merely a suggestion that perhaps there's more to the story than we've been led to believe. The prevailing version whitewashed the baseball establishment which had turned a blind eye to the gambling scandal eating away at the game.

I contend it's entirely plausible that as the start of the Series approached, the thought of playing "crooked ball" was too much for at least some of them to handle. They were "big shots" who like to talk big. "Commy" was an easy target. Here was a chance to get back at that cheap bastard, a chance to really make some dough...

But when "push came to shove," maybe they lost their nerve. Could remorse - or even panic - have set in? It wouldn't be the first time. "Could we even get away with it?" some were asking Gandil.

The entire sordid episode was a blurred, surreal sequence of events where no one really knew what anyone else was doing. A few may have cracked under the intense mental anguish, as Chick Gandil implied in his 1956 interview.

Conflicting stories and emotions were rampant. Who was trying? Who wasn't? Was it worth the risk? Was it too late to call it off? They took money. Now what? Was it too late to give it back? They made a "devil's bargain" with the gamblers. What happens when you double-cross gamblers? All this and much, much more had to be tormenting them as the opening game of the 1919 World Series approached. Who could possibly concentrate on winning baseball? On a national stage, no less. And against a great team like the Reds.

The situation was ripe for an upset...

The Black Sox were an extraordinary mix of arrogance, stupidity, naivety, greed, and, yes, talent. Conspiring with gamblers to throw the World Series was a serious offense. They got what they deserved and they knew it. The acceptance of dirty money irreversibly tarnished their reputations and made their future protestations of innocence ring hollow. As with a tar baby, once they touched the gamblers, they could never break free. Their fate was sealed.

But what really happened? It's time to reexamine the events of the 1919 World Series with "pursuit of the truth" the only goal. Let the chips fall where they may.

# Another Look at the Black Sox Scandal: Sportswriter Hugh Fullerton's "Seven Suspicious Plays

Those of you who read my last post on the Black Sox scandal, Another Look at the 1919 World Series will remember I tried to offer up some "food for thought" in that post.

I honestly don't know what really happened in that infamous Series – which we all can agree was baseball's darkest hour. I just have a hunch that the conventional wisdom doesn't quite tell us the entire story. One hundred years later, my only purpose is to take a fresh look at the known facts and try to assess the situation objectively and unemotionally. Certainly feel free to agree or disagree with me.

In the featured photo above, we see the entire 1919 White Sox team. See below for complete player identifications.

One aspect of the scandal that I've always found rather odd is the "Seven Suspicious Plays" identified by sportswriter Hugh Fullerton.

Hugh Fullerton did more than anyone else to break the story through his newspaper column in the *Chicago Herald and Examiner*, including enduring deaths threats. Rumors of a "fix" filled the air as the Series approached; so Fullerton, like many others in the press box, was observing the action with a sharp, skeptical eye. With that as his mindset, it was easy to spot what appeared to be "suspicious play." But isn't it odd that Fullerton, sitting alongside Christy Mathewson, came up with only seven for the entire eight-game series?

The most controversial of Fullerton's "seven suspicious plays" occurred in the fourth inning of Game Four, when Eddie Cicotte errantly deflected a strong throw to the plate by Joe Jackson, allowing an important run to score. It soon became conventional wisdom that it was deliberate. Those looking for evidence of "crooked play" always cite this as "Exhibit A."

But Chick Gandil claimed that he was yelling at Eddie to cut off the throw, viewing it as the proper play. And here's the real kicker: "Clean Sox" Eddie Collins, the future Hall-of-Famer, saw it first-hand from his position at second base. He later backed Cicotte, saying the attempted cut-off was indeed the correct play. A few batters earlier, Eddie had himself made a great play on a ball hit up the middle by Morrie Rath. Even catcher Ray Schalk said Eddie gave his best all the way.

Another of Fullerton's disputed plays involved Shano

Collins, who was never accused of anything. One involved Risberg backing up on an infield single; another had Williams going into a streak of wildness in the fourth inning of Game Two; two others were mound misplays by Cicotte, who was not known to be a good fielder. His .942 fielding average is the thirty-sixth worst all-time.

And that's it. What World Series has never had a few miscues, errors, or streaks of wildness? None of these seven plays directly involved Chick Gandil, the so-called ring leader, or even Happy Felsch. Most objective historians clear Jackson and Weaver from crooked play. McMullin had only two at-bats, going one-for-two, and never touched the ball. So just who was doing all the 'fixing'? When did they do it?

If you read my previous post, you'll remember that other eye-witnesses, including the official scorer and the umpires on the field, thought the Series was played "on the level."

Are we to believe that these seven plays alone resulted in a "thrown" eight-game World Series? I guess it's possible that the Eight Men Out were such good actors that they could somehow pull it off; and baseball lifers, watching closely for crooked play, wouldn't even notice. But, in the confused mental state they were in, somehow I tend to doubt it.

Here's a reprint of the conclusion from my previous post:

"In the days before the start of the 1919 World Series, the entire sordid episode became a blurred, surreal sequence of events where no one really knew what anyone else was doing or thinking. A few may have cracked under the intense mental stress, as Chick

Gandil implied in his 1956 interview.

Conflicting stories and emotions were rampant. Was it really worth the risks? Who was trying? Who wasn't? Was it too late to call it off? They took money. Now what? Was it too late to give it back? They made a "devil's bargain" with the gamblers. What happens when you double-cross gamblers? All this and much, much more had to be mentally tormenting them as the opening game of the World Series approached. Who could possibly concentrate on winning baseball? On a national stage, no less. And against a great team like the Reds.

The situation was ripe for an upset…

The Black Sox were an extraordinary mix of arrogance, stupidity, naivety, greed, and, yes, talent. Conspiring with gamblers to throw the World Series was a serious offense. They got what they deserved and they knew it. The acceptance of dirty money irreversibly tarnished their reputations and made their future protestations of innocence ring hollow. ("We took their money but we double-crossed them by trying to win." Right...Who's going to believe that?) Their fate was sealed. As with a tar baby, once they touched the gamblers, they could never break free."

Again, I don't know what really happened. I only offer this up as more "food for thought." But are you starting to feel, as I do, that perhaps there's more to this sad story than meets the eye?

## 1919 White Sox Player Identifications

Top Row, L-R: Kid Gleason(Mgr.), John Sullivan (P),

Roy Wilkinson (P), Grover Lowdermilk (P), Swede Risberg (SS), Fred McMullin (3B), Bill James (P), Eddie Murphy (OF), Joe Jackson (OF), Joe Jenkins (C). Middle Row, L-R: Ray Schalk (C), Shano Collins (OF), Red Faber (P), Dickie Kerr (P), Hap Felsch (CF), Chick Gandil (1B), Buck Weaver (3B). Front Row, L-R: Eddie Collins (2B), Nemo Liebold (OF), Eddie Cicotte (P), Erskine Mayer (P), Lefty Williams (P), Byrd Lynn (C).

# Another Look at the 1919 Black Sox Scandal: Eddie Cicotte's Performance in Game One

"I did it for the wife and kiddies." -Eddie Cicotte[56]

Those of you following my recent posts about the 1919 World Series know that my only point has been that I have my doubts that the "conventional wisdom" is telling us the whole story. So I've been offering up some "food for thought," uncovering oddities from the Series that just don't seem to add up, while trying to make sense of the whole sordid affair. My last post showed that many of the eye-witness accounts don't seem to jive with the accepted version. Here's another one along those same lines.

Take, for instance, Eddie Cicotte's performance in Game One. After taking a good look at it, I've found it raises questions that don't have easy answers, especially since the "conventional wisdom" tells us that the first two games were definitely thrown.

[56] Source information and quotes for this essay from *Burying the Black Sox*

The Reds were the home team. The game was played on October 1, 1919, at Cincinnati's Redland Field in front of 30,511 fans. As the ace of the staff, Eddie was slated by manager Kid Gleason to pitch the Opener. He was coming off a phenomenal year, going 29-7 (.806), with a 1.82 ERA, leading the league in wins, winning percentage, and complete games with 30.

The White Sox took a shellacking, losing 9-1; so it's always been assumed that Eddie intentionally "threw" this game, or at least didn't give it his best effort.

It's generally accepted that by hitting the first batter, Morrie Rath, with the second pitch of the game, Eddie gave the signal that the fix was on. Of course, that raises an interesting question about the *first* pitch, a called strike fastball. What if Rath had swung and hit it? What then? What would happen to the "signal"? We'll set that question aside for the moment, as we address other issues.

Author Victor Luhr made an interesting point in his 1966 book *The Great Baseball Mystery*, suggesting Eddie played to win after that first batter; but added: "He was in such bad mental shape as a result of his involvement in the scandal that he was hardly fit to pitch the opener."

That statement fits nicely with the conclusion I've written in previous posts:

"In the days before the start of the 1919 World Series, the entire sordid episode became a blurred, surreal sequence of events where no one really knew what anyone else was doing or thinking. A few may have cracked under the intense mental stress, as

Chick Gandil implied in his 1956 interview with *The Sporting News*."

There's no doubt that Eddie was heavily involved with the planning of the fix. Some say he, along with Chick Gandil, was a ringleader. It's also pretty certain that Eddie pocketed a cool ten grand before the series started. He clearly had a motive: He was making half of what he was worth. But by the time the Series started, Eddie was deeply remorseful, possibly more so than any of the others, and was mentally anguished by his actions. He was the first to "come clean" in his tearful testimony before the grand jury that broke open the floodgates to the scandal.

Anyway, back to the first game…

The Reds pushed Rath across and took an early 1-0 lead. The White Sox came back and tied the game in the second off Dutch Ruether. That's how the game stood going into the fateful bottom of the fourth when the roof caved. But was it Eddie's fault? Read on and decide for yourself.

The inning started innocently enough with Edd Roush flying out to Felsch in deep center. The next batter, Pat Duncan, then singled to right. One on, one out.

Now here's where it got interesting: Eddie then made what was described as a "dazzling" defensive play, fielding a hot shot off the bat of Larry Kopf. Eddie made an accurate throw to shortstop Swede Risberg to force Duncan at second. But Risberg's relay to Gandil was late by an eyelash, costing Eddie an inning-ending double play. Two outs, man on first.

Eddie *again* appeared to have the third out when the next batter, Greasy Neale, hit a lazy pop fly to short left. Risberg went back on the ball, had it in his glove, but failed to hold on. As Victor Luhrs described the play:

"No error was charged, but Eddie really had gotten his man. Given the extra outs, the Reds took advantage and went on to rout the White Sox, *scoring five runs after two outs,* and Eddie was out of the game. In sportswriter I.E. Sanborn's *Chicago Tribune* account, "the Reds' rally hung on the toenail of Kopf beating Risberg's throw to first.

Too bad there weren't replays and appeals back then!

Can this disastrous inning really be blamed on Eddie Cicotte? The White Sox defensive gave the Reds two extra outs; and, as a great team should, they took advantage of it. Eddie should have been out of the inning with no runs and the game tied at one. Who knows what the outcome would have been if either of these plays had been made? Would we even be talking about this Series today? Incidentally, had an error been charged, those five runs would all have been unearned, and Eddie's performance would have looked a lot better.

This fits my theme that there's more to the Series than meets the eye. The more I delve into the details, the more inconsistencies with the conventional wisdom I discover. Here's one of my favorites, as quoted by Umpire Ernie Quigley. He cited two great plays by Edd Roush and Morrie Rath:

"But for these two plays, the White Sox would have won at least two more games, which would have *meant the Series for them."*[57]

It's hard to jive the conventional wisdom with a statement like that...

A remorseful Eddie Cicotte always claimed he was trying to win after the first batter: "I pitched my best afterwards. I didn't care what happened. They could have had my heart and soul if I could have gotten out of the deal. I lost because I was hit, not because I was throwing the game." Even "Clean Sox" catcher Ray Schalk said, "Eddie gave his best all the way."

I must repeat: All this is not to excuse Eddie Cicotte or the Black Sox. Conspiring with gamblers to throw the World Series was a serious offense. They got what they deserved and they knew it. The acceptance of dirty money irreversibly tarnished their reputations and made their future protestations of innocence ring hollow.

It's just that we're trying to uncover the truth in the details…

---

[57] *The Sporting News*, October 1, 1920

# Another Look At The 1919 Black Sox Scandal:

## Shoeless Joe Jackson, Part One

## "Did Joe Confess?"

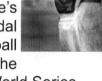

*"The Supreme Being— not Judge Landis—will be my judge. The Good Lord knows I'm innocent of any wrongdoing."* – Joe Jackson[58]

With the next series of posts, I'll focus on different aspects of Shoeless Joe's involvement in the scandal that rocked the baseball world to its core in the aftermath of the 1919 World Series.

There's probably no topic that's more emotionally charged when discussing the 1919 World Series than Joe Jackson's guilt or innocence. It's still hotly debated almost 100 years later. It's not my intent to settle the issue today; but I'll just try to present the known facts as objectively as I can, and you can make up your own mind.

Again, as I've said in each of the posts in this series,

[58] Joe Jackson information and quotes in this essay edited from *Burying the Black Sox*

this is not in any way to excuse the "Eight Men Out." They got what they deserved and they knew it. My only purpose has been to demonstrate my gut feeling that there's a lot more to the story than the conventional wisdom has led us to believe. There were certainly different levels of guilt. Those of you following these articles I think would tend to agree. I'm hoping to uncover the truth in the details of this sordid story.

Today, in Part One, I'll address the question: Did Joe Jackson "confess" to the grand jury? As you'll soon see, the answer, as with everything associated with the Black Sox scandal, is not cut-and-dry. In future articles, I'll be taking an in-depth look at his play in the field, the $5,000 he received, and the 1924 Milwaukee trial in which he sued Charles Comiskey for back pay.

So did Shoeless Joe confess to his involvement in the Black Sox scandal or not? Didn't he admit his guilt to the grand jury?

The short answer is "yes," but read on…

The floodgates to the scandal broke with Eddie Cicotte's tearful confession to the grand jury on September 28, 1920, a statement, it should be noted, he later recanted. At the time, there were still three games still left in the 1920 season and the White Sox were only a half game out of first place.

Next came Joe Jackson. You can easily make the case that the barely-literate Jackson, visibly under the influence of alcohol, was coached into making a statement to the grand jury by Charles Comiskey's lawyer, Alfred Austrian. It was a statement that was very detrimental to himself while beneficial to

Comiskey. Along with the acceptance of dirty money, nothing has been more damaging to his reputation than this supposed confession. It overrides his outstanding performance on the field, where he hit .375, hit the only home run of the Series, and played errorless ball in the field.

You can also make the case that Jackson knew what he was doing when he testified, admitted being aware of the plot, said he "let up some," and took $5,000 of money provided by gamblers. He hoped that by "confessing" he'd avoid indictment and further legal problems.

So which was it?

There's no debating that Joe made a statement to the grand jury on September 28, 1920 that came to be characterized in the media the next day as a confession. Joe met with Austrian after he learned he had been implicated by Cicotte. He was coerced by Austrian into signing away his immunity, something he didn't realize he was doing; and he acted without benefit of legal counsel. He was also coached by Austrian as to what to say. He then went voluntarily to the grand jury with the intent, he thought, of clearing his name.

To put it mildly, Joe was "out of his league" when it came to legal matters and was vulnerable to coercion. He trusted Alfred Austrian. According to Gene Carney in *Burying the Black Sox*:

"Afraid of being indicted, Jackson found reassurance and safety in Austrian's advice. It appears that Jackson was told to give the grand jury what they wanted, something that could be used to punish the gamblers."

So with that in mind, he followed Austrian's advice and was persuaded to talk. In his statement, he admitted agreeing to a fix with gamblers and to accepting cash, but told the grand jury he did nothing to earn it, and played all games to win. Carney further writes:

"Austrian may have advised him, in the words of Eliot Asinof, 'To deny your involvement will prejudice the grand jury. Do you understand that?' Jackson wanted to stay out of trouble. So he testified. He said he let up some. And then he said he played every game to win. *In the newspapers the next day, no one reported the latter statement. Whatever Jackson actually said, it went down as a 'confession'.*"

From here it gets even more complicated. The next day, newspapers reported that he "confessed" on the heels of Cicotte. They also said he made numerous incriminating statements, about how he "struck out in the clutch;" "just poked at the ball with men in scoring position;" and "let up in the field."

But these alleged statements appear nowhere in his grand jury testimony, and no one ever remembers him saying anything like this. Did reporters just make all this up? It's very possible, since we know the "Say it ain't so, Joe" episode is almost certainly a fabrication. In addition, the statements he did make that do appear in his grand jury testimony, about "playing every game to win, at bat and in the field," were reprinted nowhere.

Read this interesting quote from White Sox historian, Richard Lindberg:

"...Sportswriters [in those days] were topnotch story tellers but poor researchers, who recited anecdotes and yarns they heard in the press box as the gospel truth, and as a result myths and legends became facts in print that future baseball historians had to try to prove but very often could not."

Sounds like that could be the case here...

Joe Jackson admitted taking $5,000, given to him by Lefty Williams. He also denied doing anything to earn it. Here's a portion of what he said, the part of his testimony that went unreported:

1. Did you make any intentional errors yourself that day (Game Four)?"
2. No, sir, not during the whole Series."
3. Did you bat to win?
4. Yes.
5. And run the bases to win?
6. Yes, sir.
7. And fielded the balls in the outfield to win?
8. I did.

Gene Carney asks: "Why did this grand jury testimony go down as a simple confession, instead of the self-contradictory account of a confused witness?"

Probably the best explanation lies in the fact that many of the local and national press corps were cronies and drinking buddies of Charles Comiskey – members of the famous *Woodland Bards*, and had a vested interest in protecting the baseball establishment, most especially Charles Comiskey. The press kept the focus on the players, not those who owned and ran baseball. So Jackson's testimony served nicely as a "confession."

Here's Gene Carney's summary:

"Testifying before the Cook County grand jury,

Jackson told two stories, and they contradicted each other, and no one asked him to choose one or the other. So both are on the record, giving fuel to those who believe he was in on the fix and to those who believe he was not."[59]

But later, in the 1924 court proceedings when Jackson sued Comiskey for back pay: "A sober Jackson was crystal clear about his performance. And he went to his grave without ever changing his story again."

Are you as confused as I am? Feel free to draw your own conclusions....

---

[59] Quotes and source information for this essay from Burying the Black Sox

# Another Look At The 1919 Black Sox Scandal

## Shoeless Joe Jackson, Part Two:

## Joe's Play in the Field

"You know, he was such a remarkable hitter it was almost impossible for him to swing without meeting the ball solidly." -Teammate Dickie Kerr, speaking of Joe Jackson[60]

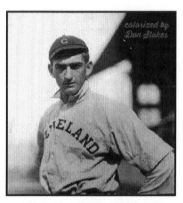

Today, in another chapter in my on-going series of essays about the 1919 World Series, I'd like to address Shoeless Joe Jackson's play and determine how it relates to his involvement (or non-involvement) in the scandal. As is well known, he hit a Series-leading .375 with six RBIs. He hit the only home run in the Series, and played errorless ball, handling 16 chances flawlessly and throwing a runner out at the plate.

In the featured photo, we see a beautiful colorization of Shoeless Joe Jackson by our resident baseball artist, Don Stokes.

Criticism aimed at him usually runs something like

[60] Quotes and source information for this essay from *Burying the Black Sox*

this:

"In the first five games, he came to bat with eleven men on base and never drove in a run. In the last three games, when the fix was apparently off, he drove in six runs and hit the only Series home run. He didn't hit in the clutch in the first five games."

If you find that criticism valid, then you have to accept the assertion that ballplayers can "pick and choose" when they want to perform well. As baseball fans, we know that just isn't so. Many great players have had less-than-stellar World Series performances, including Ty Cobb, Babe Ruth, Ted Williams, Stan Musial and Gil Hodges. You could easily add more to the list. The World Series by nature is a pressure cooker played in the national stoplight. Many stars have struggled, while obscure players have often inexplicably emerged as heroes. That's just baseball.

Keeping in mind the argument Jackson "let up" in the games that were tossed (supposedly the first two games), here's how he did in Game Two:

He went 3-for-4, with a Texas leaguer behind second that he hustled into a double; a hard single to left; and a hard smash to right that the first baseman, Jake Daubert, knocked down, then threw late to pitcher Slim Sallee, with a hustling Jackson beating the play. Does that sound like he was "laying down" in a game he knew the White Sox were trying to throw?

Let's also take a look at the play of two other stars and see if the same argument holds up against them: Player "A" went 2-for-18 (.111) in the first five games of the Series, failing to score or drive in a single run. But in the last three games, after the fix was supposedly off, he went 5-for-13 (.385), with two runs and an RBI. Player "B" went 2-for-15 (.133) in the first five games, but 4-for-13 (.308) with three runs, two doubles, and four RBI in the last three.

If you want to hold these players to the same standards some critics hold Joe Jackson, then perhaps we should examine the play of Eddie Collins (Player "A") and Edd Roush (Player "B"). [This idea came from baseball researcher Bill Deane in e-mail exchange with Gene Carney]

As for his fielding, the criticism goes like this:

"Jackson was not charged with any errors in the Series, but he played out of position, he let balls fall in for hits, and three of the Reds' triples went to left field where triples are rare."

But in all the official accounts of the game, Jackson's name is nowhere mentioned in any descriptions of the triples. Gene Carney asks: "Was he playing out of position, or was he playing where he should have been if the pitchers were trying for outs, and not tossing up hittable pitches?"

There's no way to know for sure. But read this quote from Kid Gleason describing an incident in 1917 that surely would have held in 1919 when he was the manager:

"If there had been anything wrong, I would have known it. I knew everything that went on around the club." It seems likely that Gleason would have spotted anyone playing out of position and moved them correctly. Would Gleason have just sat idly by and allowed Jackson to 'play out of position' in World Series games?

In addition, none of the 'Seven Suspicious Plays' spotted by sportswriter Hugh Fullerton, who was actively looking for anything out of the ordinary, involved Joe Jackson, either in the field, on the bases, or at the plate.

I think we can put the 'he played out of position' notion to rest.

For that matter, other than Fullerton, none of the reporters covering the Series for the Chicago and New York papers, as well as the wire services, wrote about any plays that looked suspicious. Even reporters who were pretty sure the fix was on could not be certain. Nor did the umpires or the Official Scorer observe anything untoward. Thousands of fans watched the 1919 World Series in person and saw nothing unusual. Why? As Gene Carney writes in Burying the Black Sox:

"Because that's the nature of baseball. Players trying their best still make errors. The best hitters can strike out in the clutch, the best pitchers can lose their effectiveness and look awful for an inning or two. If you are convinced that the 'fix is in' you will find suspicious plays in any ballgame. If you are not on the lookout, you will not see anything except 'baseball'."

In summary, Joe Jackson's play in the World Series was, on the surface, exceptional. He hit well against a staff rated better than that of the White Sox by Christy Mathewson. He hit safely in six of the eight games, with five multi-hit games. He fanned just twice in 32 trips to the plate and he fielded 16 chances flawlessly. Again, quoting from Gene Carney:

"To suggest that he intentionally hit better in certain

games than in others is to suggest that he could rack up hits at will, whenever he wanted, which is ridiculous. Batters can look awful in 'Homerun Derby,' when the pitchers are serving up whatever the batter wants. But even accomplished hitters make outs more often than they get hits, and often the outs come in the clutch."

Sadly, all this does not make a definite case for Joe Jackson's honest play. It's just one way of looking at the facts. As with all aspects of the 1919 World Series, nothing is cut-and-dry; but on the surface, it's very difficult to say that Joe Jackson did not play hard the entire Series: at bat, in the field, and on the bases; and that he played every game to win, as he maintained throughout the rest of his life.

Of course all this begs the question: If we are reasonably certain that Joe Jackson played hard and played to win the entire Series, does it really matter if he gave a contradictory statement to the grand jury, while under the influence of alcohol and after being coached by Comiskey lawyer, Alfred Austrian, and without benefit of personal legal counsel? A statement he later refuted? If he did accept money, does it really matter if, as he always maintained, he did nothing to earn it on the field?

It was a huge mistake for him to accept tainted money, making his later protestations of innocence much harder for even his supporters to swallow; but if someone wanted to give him money, did he really have a moral obligation not to accept it as long as he didn't let it influence his actions? He also claimed he tried to inform Comiskey about it, and tried to give the money to either Secretary Harry Grabiner or Comiskey, but was rebuffed and told to keep it.

When he testified to this in the 1924 Milwaukee trial in which he sued Comiskey for back pay, 11 of the 12 jurors believed his version of events rather than Charles Comiskey's.

Could it be, as he and others have maintained, that the gamblers and the ringleaders wanted his name associated with the "fix" so as to give an air of credibility? In that sense, was it worth it to them to have Joe compromised by giving him money? This suggestion was given credence by Lefty Williams' testimony in the 1924 Milwaukee trial when he said under oath that he "used Jackson's name in the meetings with the gamblers [meetings Jackson did not attend] without Jackson's knowledge or permission."

Jackson also claimed Williams told him "he used my name in order to wring more money out of certain fellows supposed to be gamblers." In other words, his name and his celebrity status as a star player might have been useful to the plot whether or not he was an active participant. The gamblers could spread the word that "Jackson's in on it;" and, as a key player, that most certainly would have affected the odds.

I think these are all questions worth further investigation when considering Joe Jackson's role in the 1919 World Series. Again, I don't know what really happened. I just think, after the passage of 100 years, the whole sordid mess deserves a closer look; and that the conventional wisdom does not tell us the complete story.

# Another look at the 1919 Black Sox Scandal

## Shoeless Joe Jackson, Part Three:

## Joe and the Tainted $5,000

"There are things in this world to be regarded above money – keeping faith in your friends, for instance. All of which goes to show that you don't have to know how to read and write to be a man of principle and conscience." –Joe Jackson[61]

In today's essay I'll address the question of whether Joe Jackson took $5,000 of the gamblers' money and what it means to his involvement in the plot to throw the 1919 World Series.

Like everything else associated with the Black Sox scandal, the issue is confusing and can be interpreted numerous ways, adding fuel to partisans on both sides.

**Did Joe Jackson receive $5,000 from the gamblers?**

---

[61] Quotes in this essay from Burying the Black Sox, except where indicated.

The short answer is "yes."

**Who gave him the money?**

Teammate and friend Lefty Williams.

**Did accepting the $5,000 from Lefty Williams in a "dirty envelope" hurt his reputation?**

Yes, it was a huge mistake, as it made his later protestations of innocence much harder to swallow, for even his most staunch supporters.

**When did he receive the money?**

He told two versions. In his 1920 grand jury testimony, he said he got it after Game Four or Five; in the 1924 Milwaukee trial, in which he sued the White Sox for back pay, he said he got it after the last game.

**Why did Lefty Williams say he gave Joe the money?**

Williams said he used Joe's name to get more money from the gamblers, and then felt for this reason that he "owed" it to Joe. One explanation holds that Joe's status as a celebrity and a star player was beneficial to the plotters whether or not he was an active participant. They wanted his name associated with the fix to give it more credibility. In that sense, it may have been worth it to them to have Joe compromised by giving him money. The gamblers could spread the word that "Jackson's in on it"; and, as a key player, that most certainly would have affected the odds.

This notion was given credence in Lefty Williams' testimony in the 1924 Milwaukee trial when he said under oath that he "used Jackson's name in the meetings with the gamblers [meetings Joe did not

122

attend] without Jackson's knowledge or permission."
Jackson also claimed Williams told him "he used my
name in order to wring more money out of certain
fellows supposed to be gamblers."

## What is Joe's explanation as to why he got the money?

He doesn't know why it was given to him, other than
the gamblers and plotters wanted him associated
with the fix. He always claimed he did nothing to
earn it. He played his best the entire Series, and his
stellar play proved it.

## What was Joe's first action after he received the money?

He said he made attempts see White Sox owner
Charles Comiskey and Secretary Harry Grabiner to
give them the money or at least inform them as to
what had transpired. He claimed he was rebuffed in
these efforts and was told to keep the money. There
is no solid evidence that he made the attempt to
see Comiskey, only Joe's word. The evidence for
the Grabiner rebuff is much stronger. At the 1924
Milwaukee trial, 11 of the 12 jurors believed Joe on
this point.

## What did Joe say about the money in the 1924 Milwaukee trial?

He reiterated his claim that he tried to see Comiskey
and Grabiner as soon as he received the money. He
gave this explanation as to why it was given to him
and why he took it: "He [Williams] didn't want the
money, and I thought just this way, since that lousy
so-called gambling outfit had used my name, I might
as well have their money as for him [Williams]."

**What did Joe do with the money?**

There are differing accounts, but they all seem to point in the same direction: that Joe viewed the money as "tainted."

According to biographer Donald Gropman: "Neither Joe nor his wife Katie believed the money was theirs, to spend on themselves. They put it in savings and let it earn interest. After Katie death, it was donated to the American Heart Fund and the American Cancer Society."[62]

In the 1924 Milwaukee trial, Katie also said that she used some of it trying to save Joe's sister Gertrude, who was hospitalized. Gene Carney makes an interesting point: "Some believe it is more likely that he regarded money the old-fashioned way, as something you *earned*; so because in his mind he had done nothing to earn this money, it was tainted, and he was reluctant to spend it except to help others."

**If he did accept the money, does it really matter if, as he always maintained, he did nothing to earn it on the field? In other words, was he under a moral obligation *not* to accept the money, no matter what?**

Again, it was a huge mistake for him to accept tainted money. It was damaging to his reputation and made his later protestations of innocence much harder to believe. But if someone wanted to give him money, after his name had been illicitly dragged into the plot, did he have an obligation *not* to accept it as long as he didn't allow it to influence his actions? In his defense, most objective historians conclude he

---

[62] *Burying the Black Sox*, p. 72

played to win the entire Series; so whether it was the right moral decision or not, the money apparently *did not* influence his play.

## Can you shed more light on the 1924 Milwaukee trial?

In the trial, in which Jackson sued the White Sox for back pay, the jury were given questions to address regarding the $5,000 and Jackson's involvement. Some of these questions included:

1. "Did Lefty Williams give Jackson the money before all the games in the Series were played?" The jury responded 11-1, "No."

2. "At the time Williams gave Jackson the money, did he tell Jackson that there had been an agreement between certain ballplayers to lose or 'throw' the games, and that the $5,000 was his [Jackson's] share of the money received by the players for their part in the agreement?" They responded 11-1, "No."

3. "Did Joe Jackson unlawfully conspire with Gandil, Williams, and other members of the White Sox Club, or any of them, to lose or 'throw' any of the baseball games of the 1919 World Series to the Cincinnati Baseball club?" Again, they responded 11-1, "No."

4. Did Harry Grabiner mislead Joe Jackson about the reserve clause and thus Jackson was entitled to his back pay? The jury responded 11-1 in Jackson's favor.

These were all points disputed by Comiskey; and the jury, after considering all the evidence and listening

125

to Joe's words, his tone of voice, and watching his facial expressions, decided in his favor. In his testimony, Comiskey conceded that Joe had played all the games of the 1919 World Series to win.

Charles Comiskey's grandson has sworn that the Comiskey family's belief was that "Jackson neither conspired to throw nor attempted to throw any or all games in the 1919 World Series." **It should be noted the judge in the trial set aside the jury verdict and the case was settled out of court.**

**Did the White Sox management have a vested interest in seeing Joe indicted or compromised?**

Yes, because, he was in a unique position to expose Comiskey's effort to cover-up the scandal after he was informed about it.

Writer William Herzog: "What made the situation dangerous was the simple fact that the circumstances and facts that exonerated Jackson condemned Comiskey."[63]

Chicago lawyer David Carlson: "It's my theory that Alfred Austrian and Comiskey wanted Jackson to confess so they could compromise him. Jackson was in the unique position of substantially embarrassing Comiskey by telling of his attempts to inform him of the fix. If Jackson were indicted, however, he would be discredited. I think the evidence supports this theory."

**Does all the foregoing prove Joe's innocence in the plot?**

Sadly no. There are many ways to interpret the above information. Bottom line: Joe took the money

---

[63] "From Scapegoat to Icon," William Herzog, 2002

and kept it. In his defense, White Sox management may have instructed him to keep it after he brought to their attention. But all accounts seem to point in the direction that he did not spend it on himself as he regarded it as unearned and tainted.

## What's the Final Word?

There's probably no topic that's more emotionally charged when discussing the 1919 World Series than Joe Jackson's guilt or innocence. It's still hotly debated almost 100 years later. It was not my intent to settle the issue today; only to present the known facts involving his acceptance of the $5,000 as objectively as I could.

If you thought Joe was innocent before reading this, you are now probably even more convinced. Likewise, if you thought he was guilty, probably nothing has changed your mind.

"What all this says about the cover-up of the scandal, and Joe Jackson's character, is a matter of interpretation – and fuel for the hot stove!" –Gene Carney[64]

---

[64] Quotes and source information for this essay from *Burying the Black Sox*

# Was Buck Weaver Treated Fairly by Judge Landis?

With the 2019 World Series just around the corner, here's one more look at the 1919 Black Sox scandal, this time turning the spotlight on Buck Weaver and asking the question whether he received just punishment.

"Buck Weaver simply loved to play ball. Why he's got a smile on his face all the time, no matter what is happening. Buck is just as much a kid today as he was when he first came to the White Sox in 1912. Weaver never gives up. [65]

-Kid Gleason

If there is a case to be made for reinstatement of any of the "Eight Men Out" banned for life by Judge Landis in the aftermath of the 1919 Black Sox scandal, it would be for Buck Weaver. Certainly much can be said for Shoeless Joe Jackson who played flawlessly in the field and led all batters with a .375 average. But unfortunately for Jackson, his grand jury statement, reported as a "confession," and his acceptance of tainted money—whatever innocent explanations there might be—forever made his later claims of innocence ring hollow. They are difficult hurdles for even his most ardent supporters to overcome.

In the case of Buck Weaver, there are no such obstacles. There was no confession, no acceptance of money. In addition, none of the "Seven Suspicious

---

[65] *Burying the Black Sox*, p. 210

Plays" recorded by sportswriter Hugh Fullerton involved Weaver. There has never been any suggestion that he gave less than one hundred percent the entire Series, hitting .324 (11-43), and fielding flawlessly. His play was so solid and inspirational that it prompted this appraisal from Cincinnati sportswriter Ross Tenney, hardly an unbiased observer, shortly after the Series ended:

> "Though they are hopeless and heartless, the White Sox have a hero. He is George Weaver, who plays and fights at third base. Day after day Weaver has done his work and smiled. In spite of the certain fate that closed about the hopes of the Sox, Weaver smiled and scrapped. One by one his mates gave up. Weaver continued to grin and fought harder....Weaver's smile never faded. His spirit never waned....The Reds have beaten the spirit out of the Sox all but Weaver. Buck's spirit is untouched. He was ready to die fighting. Buck is Chicago's one big hero; long may he fight and smile."[66]

So just why was Buck banned? As the conventional wisdom tells us, Buck apparently either sat in on one or two early meetings where the conspiracy was first hatched; or at some point was informed of the plan. But he never consented to it, never agreed to participate, and only possessed "guilty knowledge," in the famous words of Judge Landis.

Put simply, he declined to squeal on his teammates. Perhaps this decision can be most easily explained by the fact he was apparently threatened with physical violence by Gandil and Risberg if he talked, two guys

---

[66] Buck Weaver SABR Bioproject article  by David Fletcher

the 5'11", 170 pound Weaver understandably didn't want to cross.

For keeping quiet, Buck was lumped in with the others and received the same one-size-fits-all lifetime ban from Landis. Was he the only one who had prior inklings of a fix? That seems hard to believe, but he became a convenient scapegoat. Gene Carney makes the following point:

"Landis, by keeping the focus on a minimum number of players [including Weaver], was doing exactly what the owners (especially Comiskey, who had a large hand in hiring Landis) wanted. Baseball's image would suffer no more than it had already. Management's role, *baseball's* role in covering up the ties between the sport and gambling, was not to be explored."[67]

Sportswriter Hugh Fullerton, who did more than anyone to break the story, once stated that "not fewer than a hundred ballplayers had information that something was doing when the Series started."[68]

Here's what Buck had to say about his so-called "guilty knowledge":

> "The only doubt in my mind, was whether I should keep quiet about it or tell Mr. Comiskey. I was not certain just what men, if any, had received propositions or whether they had accepted. I couldn't bring myself to tell on them even had I known for certain. I decided to keep quiet and play my best."[69]

[67] *Burying the Black Sox,* p. 213
[68] *Atlanta Constitution,* July 16, 1921
[69] *New York Times,* January 14, 1922

This nicely makes my point that there were different levels of involvement in this sordid affair. Should Weaver have received the same sentence as those who actively conspired with gamblers to throw the Series, took money, and may have thrown games? I hardly think so, and neither did many others. From our vantage point one hundred years later, it seems that a suspension, possibly for a year, would have been a more appropriate sentence.

Fixer Abe Attell always maintained Weaver was guiltless, and once tried to persuade Landis to reinstate him. "The kid didn't get a dime out of it, and he didn't know what was going on, either."[70] Writer Damon Runyon once interceded with Landis on Buck's behalf but was rebuffed with the same "guilty knowledge" assertion.

Here's other observations:

Nelson Algren: "The verdict we once applauded as one of Olympian sagacity was nothing more, it has become plain, than a legal mugging by an enraptured Puritan. Weaver is punished ruthlessly while the silence of Comiskey with equal knowledge of corruption, deserved only praise."[71]

James T. Farrell: "The two players I have sympathy for are Weaver and Joe Jackson. They were brought up in an environment where you were not supposed to squeal. What could they have done?"[72]

Buck Weaver applied for reinstatement six times before his death in Chicago on January 31, 1956 at age 65. He was the third of the banned Black Sox to

---

[70] *The Joe Williams Baseball Reader*
[71] *The Last Carousel*, by Nelson Algren
[72] *My Baseball Diary*, by James T. Farrell

pass away, following Joe Jackson in 1951 and Fred McMullin in 1952. One notable but failed attempt occurred in the wake of the Tris Speaker/Ty Cobb betting scandal. Later in life, Weaver contacted a New York attorney who claimed he could get him reinstated. Buck sent him his legal papers but they were never returned and their whereabouts are unknown to this day.

In *Burying the Black Sox*, Gene Carney summarizes the plight of Buck Weaver, citing one of the saddest of baseball documents, which is on display at the National Baseball Museum in Cooperstown—a letter from Buck Weaver to Commissioner Ford Frick in 1953:

> "At age sixty-three, (he would die three years later), Buck was still trying to clear his name with Major League Baseball. He insisted that he 'knew nothing' and 'played a perfect Series.' When he sued his team, after he was banned from baseball, contending that he deserved the pay for the last year of his contact (1921), he won, which proved in Buck's view that he was right and Comiskey was wrong."[73]

Chicago Tribune columnist Mike Downey wrote a column in 2005 calling for Weaver's reinstatement. He cited catcher Ray Schalk's insistence that there were actually only seven players involved, excluding Buck. In recent years, several members of Weaver's family, including nieces Pat Anderson and Marjorie Follet took up the case for their uncle's reinstatement. They made unsuccessful appeals to then-commissioner Bud Selig. Both have since passed away. The torch has fallen to a new

---

[73] *Burying the Black Sox*, p. 211

generation of the Weaver family, grand-nieces Debra Ebert and Sandy Schley. Both appeared at a recent symposium on the Black Sox scandal sponsored by the Chicago chapter of the Society for American Baseball Research (SABR).

To answer my original question: Was Buck Weaver treated fairly by Judge Landis? Sadly, I have to conclude the answer is no. Let's hope a future commissioner will see the harm done to the reputation of this fine ballplayer and correct an egregious injustice.

# Book Review
## *Burying the Black Sox,*
## by Gene Carney

**Reviewed by Gary Livacari**

It is hard to put into words the service that author Gene Carney, with the publication of his wonderful new book *Burying the Black Sox,* has performed for all of us amateur baseball historians who are forever intrigued by the 1919 Black Sox scandal. Mr. Carney's great achievement is that he steps into the world of lies, conspiracies, gamblers, and cover-ups that pervade this sordid but fascinating chapter in baseball history, and attempts to make sense of it all.

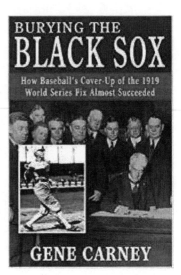

What emerges is a book that is both a joy to read and highly informative. The wealth of new information the author uncovers is simply remarkable. It's a book that is well written and edited, with just the right dose of stylistic flair and humor. It's never boring; and, quite frankly, I had trouble putting it down.

It also succeeds in capturing both the essence of the 1919 World Series scandal and the cultural flavor of post-World War I America. We see remarkable similarities to our present time. As with steroids in today's game, we sense that gambling had a death grip on the National Pastime by 1919, and was a problem festering for at least a decade. Like today's baseball hierarchy trying to deal with the problem of PEDs, many of baseball's ruling elite buried their collective heads in the sand, hoped it would just go away, and orchestrated a cover-up. It took a grand jury to get their attention. The thought of dealing with the problem in an open and forthright manner never seemed to occur to them. Like Watergate, the cover-up didn't hold, and in many ways, was worse than the crime.

Most of us are familiar with the overall picture of the Black Sox scandal, but we get lost in the morass of details. Here's where *Burying the Black Sox* is a real help. How many of us conflate the 1920 Grand Jury "confessions" with the 1921 trial with the 1924 civil suit? The cast of characters includes a highly jumbled mix of crooked and clean ball players, baseball "magnates," fixers, reporters, commissioners, lawyers and judges.

And what about the gamblers? Who could possibly keep them all straight? Arnold Rothstein, Abe Attell, Sleepy Bill Burns, Sport Sullivan, Billy Maharg, the St. Louis group, the Chicago group, the New York group, the Des Moines group, the Montreal group. Mr. Carney has earned a permanent niche in baseball history just for attempting to sort out this mess. He details the tangled web of gamblers and fixers in a spoof of the old Abbott and Costello "Who's on First?" routine. It's worth the price of the book itself.

And then there are the eternal questions: Who

initiated the fix? Why did the ballplayers do it? Was it Comiskey's fault because he was "cheap"? Which games were fixed? How do we know for sure they were fixed? Was it called off before the first game, as some contend? Who got money? Where did the money come from? Did the players "earn" it? What about Weaver and Shoeless Joe? Were they innocent victims?

With his characteristic attention to detail, these are all questions Mr. Carney addresses; and, although he doesn't quite answer them definitely (that's not his stated goal), he at least makes a credible effort to sort everything out. You are left with a far-better understanding of the issues, personalities, and motives than ever before.

To Mr. Carney's credit, he enters into the fray with no biases. He states in the preface that his goal is simply to present the facts as clearly and accurately as possible, and then let readers make up their own minds. He succeeds in this goal. Even with a topic as emotionally charged as Shoeless Joe Jackson's guilt or innocence, he dispassionately presents all the evidence, both pro and con. One gets the feeling that this is the way history books should treat Shoeless Joe; but, unfortunately, very rarely do.

A highlight of the book is the prominence Mr. Carney gives to the often-overlooked 1924 civil suit brought by Joe Jackson against Charles Comiskey for breach of his 1920 contract. Characterized by Mr. Carney as "The Trial Nobody Watched," it's hard to believe that an event so pivotal to the drama of the 1919 Black Sox scandal has gone largely unexamined. At this trial, Mr. Carney states, "For the first time, there would be new light shed on what Comiskey knew and when he knew it and on exactly what he did or did not do about it. Here for the first time, Jackson's play in the World Series would be scrutinized and whether or not he had willingly lent his name to the conspiracy."

In many ways, this trial pitted Jackson's word versus Comiskey's, with a verdict to be rendered by a jury who had access to all available evidence. They could look into the eyes of the defendants and plaintiff, listen to cross-examination, observe body language and intonation, and decide for themselves whose version was closest to the truth. Mr. Carney believes it's highly significant that—where ten votes were needed for Jackson to win his case— he got eleven: "Eleven of twelve jurors believed Jackson had played every game to win. And that he had not received the $5000 from Williams until the Series was over. And that he had not been in on the conspiracy. And that he deserved his back pay."

We also learn from reporter Frank G. Menke of some of the admissions made by Comiskey at this trial: "His $10,000 reward for information was a bluff, as it was made after he knew the Series was crooked, who was in on the fix, and practically all of the details. He admitted at the trial that he knew the identity of the crooked players two days after the Series but made no attempt to get signed statements, and permitted them to play in 1920. He admitted that Jackson played all games to win." Menke concludes that Comiskey had engineered a cover-up of the fix, and that it nearly succeeded.

So Shoeless Joe was innocent, right? Unfortunately for Jackson, the jury verdict was overturned by Judge Gregory, who could not overlook the contradictions with his 1920 statement to the Cook County grand jury (a statement wrongly characterized in the media at the time as a "confession"). It's obvious that Mr. Carney finds this jury verdict significant, but he stops well short of exonerating Joe Jackson.

Another interesting chapter is devoted to the bizarre sequence of events that led to the unraveling of the fix through the grand jury process. We learn who helped the investigation along and who hindered it. Many will be surprised to learn one of the pivotal events in this chain was a completely meaningless game in August, 1920 between the Phillies and, of all teams, the Cubs. In addition, we learn that the origin of gambling in baseball certainly did not start with the 1919 Black Sox, as many would have us believe.

Along the way we are treated to many of the often overlooked but juicy details of the case. A small sampling would include:

A description of the life-and-death power struggle between Charles Comiskey and Ban Johnson, how it led directly to the formation of the grand jury, and the possible real motives behind Johnson's desire to convene it.

The courageous role played by whistle blower Hugh Fullerton, who, with amazing parallels to the Watergate scandal, assumes the role of Woodward and Bernstein. We learn how his diligence almost single-handedly broke through the cover-up, how his efforts were nearly thwarted, and the steep price he paid to career and person, including attempted murder, for challenging baseball's ruling authorities.

The previously unheralded role played by the

gambling publication, "Collyer's Eye," its reporter Frank O. Klein, and how they tried to blow the whistle on the fix and the cover-up in the months immediately after the Series.

A detailed discussion of Judge Landis and his famous ruling that resulted in "eight men out." It succeeded in cleaning up baseball's tarnished image, but in the words of Mr. Carney, "By failing to give consideration to the different degrees of participation in the fix and by pretending that banning eight players solved the whole problem, [did] baseball officialdom perpetuate a cover-up?"

An interesting section on the "Woodland Bards": a select group of Comiskey cronies that consisted of friends, fellow owners, former ballplayers, reporters, politicians, entertainers, gamblers, and drinking buddies and the role they played in the drama.

How the media distorted Jackson's original grand jury statement, characterizing it as a "confession" instead of a "contradictory account of a confused witness," neglecting to reveal that he repeatedly stated that he played all games to win.

After years of reading about the 1919 World Series, all the events in this sordid affair are finally starting to fall into place and to make sense, thanks largely to Mr. Carney and *Burying the Black Sox*. It would be hard to call this book the "definitive" version of the Black Sox scandal, only because, as Mr. Carney states, it raises as many new questions as it answers. But I think we can safely assume that Gene Carney is today's foremost authority on the 1919 World Series; and he is to be commended for the diligence and thoroughness that he devotes to this highly emotional, highly controversial subject. It's also safe to say that *Burying the Black Sox* is a "must-read" for anyone interested in discussing intelligently this sad chapter in baseball's long and storied history.

# CONCLUSION

Throughout this collection of essays, I have attempted to make the point that the conventional wisdom regarding the Black Sox scandal and the 1919 World Series does not tell the complete story. Certainly there is more to say than simply eight members of the heavily-favored White Sox, angry at skin-flint owner Charles Comiskey, banned together and conspired with gamblers to "throw" the World Series for a big payoff.

Then, as the story goes, their plot succeeded. The fix was in, they lost the Series, the gamblers cleaned up, and the eight Black Sox got their money, although not as much as promised. A year later, under increasing scrutiny, some decided to come clean, confessed, were acquitted in court, but were banned for life by Judge Landis.

Even if you accept this superficial version, I hope you can at least agree with me that there was, at a minimum, differing levels of guilt and involvement. A one-size-fits-all punishment, which was the verdict doled out to the eight players by Judge Landis, does not now seem warranted from our vantage point one hundred years later.

I ask you to read again these quotes from Chick Gandil, from his 1956 interview for *Sports Illustrated*, commenting about the team's state of mental disarray as the start of the World Series approached:

"I truthfully wanted to go to our manager Kid Gleason and tell him the whole story, but I knew it wouldn't be that simple. I realized that things were too involved by now to try to explain. I guess some of the others must have felt the same way, because the next morning I was called to a meeting of the eight players. Everyone was upset and there was a lot of disagreement."

*"But it was finally decided that there was too much suspicion now to throw the games without getting caught. We weighed the risk of public disgrace and going to jail against taking our chances with the gamblers by crossing them up and keeping the ten grand...Our only course was to try to win, and we were certain that we could."* [Emphasis added][74]

Granted, Gandil was a shady, unreliable character and a known liar; but I don't think his words can just be dismissed out-of-hand. As I've tried to point out with the general theme running throughout the essays, an honest assessment of much of the circumstantial evidence seems to support his claims.

I'll reiterate and elaborate upon the conclusions I've reached over the course of my study of the 1919 World Series and the Black Sox scandal. I've stated different versions of these conclusions numerous times throughout the essays:

So what really happened? No one will ever know for sure. But after reading the first-hand accounts of those involved and those who were actually there, it's my contention that In the days before the start of the1919 World Series, the entire sordid episode became a blurred, surreal sequence of events where no one really knew what anyone else was doing or thinking. A few may have cracked under

---

[74] *Sports illustrated*, September 17, 1956

the intense mental stress, as Chick Gandil implied in his interview. Conflicting stories and emotions were rampant. Here's some thoughts that had to be running through their minds:

> "Is it really worth the risks? Who's still in? Who's out? Are you even sure we're getting the dough? Is it too late to call it off? We took money. Now what? Is it too late to give it back? We made a 'devil's bargain' with gamblers. What happens when you double-cross gamblers? Can we even get away with it? There'll be thousands of people watching our every move, so how do you throw a game, anyway? Which games do we throw? I'm scared!"

All this and much, much more had to be mentally tormenting them as the crucial hour approached. Who could possibly concentrate on winning baseball with this mental baggage? On a national stage, no less, and against a strong team like the Reds.

The situation was ripe for upset...

As I've said many times, it's never been my intention to exonerate the Black Sox; but merely a suggestion that we need to uncover the truth buried deep beneath the mountain of lies, distortions, and conflicting emotions. Conspiring with gamblers is less of an offense than actually throwing games. Proper levels of guilt need to be assessed. The prevailing version whitewashed the baseball establishment, which had turned a blind eye to the gambling scandal eating away at the game. Many of the Chicago and national sportswriters were Comiskey cronies—members of the famous Woodland Bards. They had a vested

143

interest in minimizing the damage to Commy's reputation and to the baseball establishment.

I contend it's entirely plausible that as the start of the Series approached, the thought of playing "crooked ball" was too much for at least some of them to handle. They were "big shots" who like to talk big. Commy was an easy target. "Here's a chance to get back at that cheap bastard, a chance to really make some dough..."

But when push came to shove, as the time approached to take the field, could they have lost their nerve? Could remorse—or even panic—have set in? It wouldn't be the first time conspirators backed out as the reality of illicit decisions set in. With rumors of a fix flying around, it was easy to spot what appeared to be suspicious play, even if it was just poor play by pre-occupied players saddled with extreme mental baggage.

The 1919 Black Sox were an extraordinary mix of arrogance, stupidity, naivety, greed, and, yes, talent. Conspiring with gamblers to throw the World Series was a serious offense. They got what they deserved and they knew it. The acceptance of dirty money irreversibly tarnished their reputations and made their future protestations of innocence ring hollow: "We took their money but we double-crossed them by trying to win."

Yeah, right...You expect us to believe that? No, once they touched the gamblers, and money was given and accepted, their fate was sealed. As with a tar baby, they could never break totally free.

Are you starting to feel, as I do, that perhaps there's more to this sordid story than meets the eye? If so, then I've succeeded in my objective with this series of essays. Again, I don't know what really happened, but I think there's a lot more to this story than we've been led to believe. I only offer up this book as "food for thought."

I do think it's time for another look at the 1919 Black Sox with pursuit of the truth as the only goal. Let the chips fall where they may.

# The Hotel Buckminster

The plot to throw the 1919 World Series was apparently hatched at Boston's Hotel Buckminster on September 19, 1919. On that day, the White Sox had defeated the Red Sox 3-2 at Fenway Park. Later, bookmaker and gambler Sport Sullivan went to the

Hotel Buckminster as it appeared in the 1910s

room of White Sox first baseman, Chick Gandil and approached him with the idea of "fixing" the upcoming World Series, just thirteen days away, for a big payoff from Arnold Rothstein.

Gandil at first balked at the notion, saying: "Are you crazy? We could never pull off fixing the World Series." Sullivan replied: "Don't be silly. It's been pulled before and it can be again."

Hotel Buckminster as it exists today

The rest, as they say, is history.

Here's a little background information on this historic hotel [75]:

The hotel, built in 1897, is located on the triangular intersection of Beacon Street and Brookline Avenue in Kenmore Square, within one block of Fenway

[75] Information: excerpts edited from Hotel Buckminster Wikipedia page

Park. It was designed by Boston architects Winslow & Wetherell, designers of many Boston area hotels and office buildings.

In 1929, pioneer station WNAC moved to new studios inside the Hotel Buckminster, which would become the station's home for the next four decades. WNAC made history in January 1923 by linking up with New York's WEAF for the first chain broadcast, later forming the Yankee Network. A pioneer FM station was added in the late 1930s.

In the following years, WNAC converted most of its studio space into one of Boston's first television studios and began broadcasting on Channel 7 in June, 1948. For the next twenty years, WNAC operated an AM, FM and television station in the hotel basement. One of its earliest and most successful radio announcers was Fred Lang (1910-1968), hired in 1936, who read the news for Yankee network over WNAC through World War II. Lang also did Queen for a Day, the Tell-o-test Quiz Show. A portion of the building was used in the 1940s by a detachment of military police to house Italian prisoners of war during World War II.

In 1950, Boston native George Wein moved his Storyville nightclub to the ground floor of the Hotel Buckminster. A number of well-known performers, especially jazz musicians, were featured in this new venue, including Louis Armstrong, Dave Brubeck, Red Garland, Erroll Garner,

Commemorative Plaque on Hotel Buckminster

Billie Holiday, Charles Mingus, Charlie Parker, and Sarah. Many made radio broadcasts from this location, some recordings of which still survive. The space that housed Storyville is now occupied by a Pizzeria Uno restaurant.

A change in ownership in the 1960s led to the hotel being briefly renamed the Hotel St. George The building was sold to Grahm Junior College in 1968 and was renamed Leavitt Hall. A few years later, the building was sold again. After restorations, the building was renamed "Boston Hotel Buckminster" and has operated as a hotel and apartment building ever since.

The Hotel Buckminster has 132 guest rooms and suites. Much of its advertising is based on its relatively low price and its close proximity to many Boston attractions including Boston University, Charles River Reservation, the Emerald Necklace, Fenway Park, the Freedom Trail, Hynes Convention Center, the Isabella Stewart Gardner Museum, Newbury Street, and the Prudential Center. Also, the Kenmore Station subway stop is nearby.

# ABOUT THE AUTHOR

Baseball historian Gary Livacari is a long-time member of the Society for Baseball Research (SABR) who enjoys writing about baseball. His forte is identifying ballplayers in old photos. For many years he did player identifications for the Baseball Fever web site. He was also an editor for the Boston Public Library Leslie Jones Baseball Project, helping to identify ballplayers in almost 3000 photos from the 1930s and 1940s. He has written biographies for the SABR Bioproject, plus numerous articles and book reviews.

He is the co-editor of the *Old-Time Baseball Photos* Facebook page which has grown to over 75,000 followers; and he is also the developer, administrator, and editor of the *Baseball History Comes Alive* web page, which also enjoys a large following.

Gary and his wife Nancy reside in Park Ridge, Illinois. He can be contacted at: Livac2@aol.com.

# Appendix: Statistical Information

## 1919 World Series Statistics [76]

Game One, October 1: Reds 9, White Sox 1, at Cincinnati (Reds lead Series 1-0)

Game Two, October 2: Reds 4, White Sox 2, at Cincinnati (Reds lead Series 2-0)

Game Three, October 3: White 3, Reds 0, at Chicago (Reds lead Series 2-1)

Game Four, October 4: Reds 2, White Sox 0, at Chicago (Reds lead Series 3-1)

Game Five, October 6: Reds 5 White Sox 0, at Chicago (Reds lead Series 4-1)

Game Six, October 7, White Sox 5, Reds 4, at Cincinnati (Reds lead Series 4-2)

Game Seven, October 8: White Sox 4, Reds 1, at Cincinnati (Reds lead Series 4-3)

Game Eight, October 9: Reds 10, White Sox 5, at Chicago (Reds win World Series 5-3)

| Individual Batting: White Sox | | | | |
|---|---|---|---|---|
| Player | BA | AB | Hits | RBI |
| McMullin | .500 | 2 | 1 | 0 |
| Jackson | .375 | 32 | 12 | 6 |
| Weaver | .324 | 34 | 11 | 0 |
| Schalk | .304 | 23 | 7 | 2 |
| Collins, S. | .250 | 16 | 4 | 0 |
| Gandil | .233 | 30 | 7 | 5 |

[76] All statistical information from Baseball-Reference.com

| | | | | |
|---|---|---|---|---|
| Collins, E. | .226 | 31 | 7 | 1 |
| Williams | .200 | 5 | 1 | 0 |
| Felsch | .192 | 26 | 5 | 3 |
| Kerr | .167 | 6 | 1 | 0 |
| Risberg | .080 | 25 | 2 | 0 |
| Leibold | .056 | 18 | 1 | 0 |
| Cicotte | 0 | 8 | 0 | 0 |
| James | 0 | 2 | 0 | 0 |
| Lowdermilk | 0 | 1 | 0 | 0 |
| Lynn | 0 | 1 | 0 | 0 |
| Mayer | 0 | 1 | 0 | 0 |
| Murphy | 0 | 2 | 0 | 0 |
| Wilkinson | 0 | 2 | 0 | 0 |

## Individual Batting: Reds

| Player | BA | AB | Hits | RBI |
|---|---|---|---|---|
| | | | | |
| Ruether | .667 | 6 | 4 | 4 |
| Wingo | .571 | 7 | 4 | 1 |
| Magee | .500 | 2 | 1 | 0 |
| Fisher | .500 | 2 | 1 | 0 |
| Neale | .357 | 28 | 10 | 4 |
| Eller | .286 | 7 | 2 | 0 |
| Duncan | .269 | 26 | 7 | 8 |
| Daubert | .241 | 29 | 7 | 1 |
| Rath | .226 | 31 | 7 | 2 |
| Kopf | .222 | 27 | 6 | 2 |
| Roush | .214 | 28 | 6 | 7 |
| Rariden | .211 | 19 | 4 | 2 |
| Groh | .172 | 29 | 5 | 2 |
| Luque | 0 | 1 | 0 | 0 |

| | | | | |
|---|---|---|---|---|
| Ring | 0 | 5 | 0 | 0 |
| Sallee | 0 | 4 | 0 | 0 |
| Smith | 0 | 0 | 0 | 0 |

## Individual Pitching, Reds

| Pitcher | W | L | ERA | | | | |
|---|---|---|---|---|---|---|---|
| Eller | 2 | 0 | 2.00 | | | | |
| Ring | 1 | 1 | 0.64 | | | | |
| Ruether | 1 | 0 | 2.57 | | | | |
| Sallee | 1 | 1 | 1.35 | | | | |
| Fisher | 0 | 1 | 2.35 | | | | |
| Lugue | 0 | 0 | 0.00 | | | | |

## Individual Pitching, White Sox

| Pitcher | W | L | ERA | | | | |
|---|---|---|---|---|---|---|---|
| Cicotte | 1 | 2 | 2.91 | | | | |
| Kerr | 2 | 0 | 1.42 | | | | |
| Williams | 0 | 3 | 6.61 | | | | |
| Wilkinson | 0 | 0 | 3.68 | | | | |
| James | 0 | 0 | 5.79 | | | | |
| Lod'milk | 0 | 0 | 9.00 | | | | |
| Mayer | 0 | 0 | 0.00 | | | | |

# 1919 World Series Statistics [77]

| Final Standings | | | | |
|---|---|---|---|---|
| **National League** | | | | |
| | Won | Lost | Pct. | GB |
| Cincinnati | 94 | 44 | .686 | - |

[77] All statistical Information from Baseball-Reference.com

| | | | | |
|---|---|---|---|---|
| New York | 87 | 53 | .621 | 9 |
| Chicago | 75 | 65 | .536 | 21 |
| Pittsburgh | 71 | 68 | .511 | 24.5 |
| Brooklyn | 69 | 71 | .493 | 27 |
| Boston | 57 | 82 | .410 | 38.5 |
| St. Louis | 54 | 83 | .394 | 40.5 |
| Philadelphia | 47 | 90 | .343 | 47.5 |

| American League | | | | |
|---|---|---|---|---|
| | Won | Lost | Pct. | GB |
| Chicago | 88 | 52 | 0.629 | - |
| Cleveland | 84 | 55 | 0.604 | 3.5 |
| New York | 80 | 59 | 0.576 | 7.5 |
| Detroit | 80 | 60 | 0.571 | 8 |
| St. Louis | 67 | 72 | 0.482 | 20.5 |
| Boston | 66 | 71 | 0.482 | 20.5 |
| Washington | 56 | 84 | 0.4 | 32 |
| Philadelphia | 36 | 104 | 0.257 | 52 |

| Batting | | | | |
|---|---|---|---|---|
| Reds | | | White Sox | |
| Eddie Roush | .321 | | Eddie Murphy | .486 |
| Hennie Groh | .310 | | Joe Jackson | .351 |
| Jake Daubert | .276 | | Eddie Collins | .319 |
| Ivy Wingo | .273 | | Nemo Leibold | .302 |
| Larry Kopf | .270 | | Buck Weaver | .296 |

| Morrie Rath | .264 | | Fred Mc-Mullin | .294 |
|---|---|---|---|---|
| Pat Duncan | .244 | | Chick Gandil | .290 |
| Greasy Neale | .242 | | Ray Schalk | .282 |
| Bill Rariden | .216 | | Shano Collins | .279 |
| Sherry Magee | .215 | | Happy Felsch | .275 |
| Rube Bressler | .206 | | Swe. Risberg | .256 |

## Pitching

| Reds | W/L | ERA |
|---|---|---|
| Slim Sallee | 21-7 | 2.06 |
| Hod Eller | 20-9 | 2.39 |
| Dutch Ruether | 19-6 | 1.82 |
| Ray Fisher | 14-5 | 2.17 |
| Jimmy Ring | 10-9 | 2.26 |
| Dolf Luque | 9-3 | 2.63 |

| White Sox | W/L | ERA |
|---|---|---|
| Eddie Cicotte | 29-7 | 1.82 |
| Lefty Williams | 23-11 | 2.64 |
| Dickie Kerr | 13-7 | 2.88 |
| G. Lowdermilk | 5-5 | 2.79 |
| Roy Wilkinson | 1-1 | 2.05 |

## Team Fielding

| | Reds | White Sox |
|---|---|---|
| Team Fielding | .974 | .969 |

| Team Errors | 152 | 176 |
|---|---|---|
| Double Plays | 98 | 116 |

## Team Pitching

| | Reds | White Sox |
|---|---|---|
| ERA | 2.23 | 3.04 |
| Complete games | 89 | 88 |
| Shutouts | 23 | 14 |

Made in the USA
Monee, IL
03 February 2020